The SUPERNATURAL

LEM BARNEY

TO; BROTHER WARREN
THE VERY BEST OF LIFE'S
FINEST MOMENTS, LOVE, JOY,
PEACE, HEALTH, WEALTH, WELLNESS
AND HAPPINESS, ALWAYS.

Lem Barney
Pro Football '92
Hall of Fame

The Supernatural

Lem Barney

An inspirational and spiritual journey of a Hall-of-Famer who scored his greatest touchdown when he reached for God's end zone.

by Lem Barney & Gus Mollasis

Foreword by Bill Cosby

Published by
Immortal Investments Publishing
www.immortalinvestments.com
35122 W. Michigan Avenue, Wayne, Michigan 48184
1-800-475-2066

Publisher's Cataloging-In-Publication Data
(Prepared by The Donohue Group, Inc.)

Mollasis, Gus.
    The Supernatural : Lem Barney / by Gus Mollasis ; foreword by Bill Cosby. -- 1st ed.

    p. ; cm.

    ISBN:978-9723637-3-0

1. Barney, Lem. 2. Football players--United States--Biography. 3. Substance abuse--Rehabilitation. 4. Spiritual healing. 5. Clergy--Appointment, call, and election. 6. Detroit Lions (Football team) I. Cosby, Bill, 1937- II. Title. III. Title: Lem Barney.

GV939.B37 M65 2006
796.332/092/4 B   2004110579

Dedication

First and foremost, I give all glory and honor to my Lord and Savior Jesus Christ who gave me the talent and ability to achieve the dreams and desires of my heart. The Word says: "If you delight yourself in the Lord, He will give you the desires of your heart."

The story of my life is also a story of family and friends. I would like to thank them for the courage they have displayed throughout this project and the trust they placed in me. I am grateful and feel tremendously blessed for the love and generosity family and friends have demonstrated to me.

To my Mom and Dad for their love for one another and their love of God and their family. Thank you for the encouragement, support and the word of God. I will always cherish and remember your guidance to put God first, family second and remember I can do all things through Christ who strengthens me. Thank you for helping me to develop into the man I am today. Thanks for always believing in, encouraging, supporting and nurturing my dreams and aspirations. I will love you always and may your souls rest in peace.

To my wife, the love of my life, Jacci. You are the light of my life. Thank you for your prayers and always encouraging me to be the best in all of my endeavors in life. Thank you for your love and support. Thank you for the love we share for one another and the journey we are on. Thank you for a love that will last a lifetime with God on our side. I love You.

To my children, Lem III and Latrece. Thank you for always loving and respecting me as your Dad. Thanks for all of the memorable moments we have shared together. You are the joys of my life.

To my grandson, Jamir—you are my inspiration, my sunshine on a cloudy day. You are gran dad's favorite!

To my sisters, Rosemary (who's gone to glory, I will love you always), Varina and Lemelda thank you for your love, support and encouragement throughout the years. Thank you for the fun and laughter and tears we have shared together.

To my sisters in law—Dora aka (the skipster), Rose and Millie and to my brother in law, Bob—thank you for loving me like a brother and welcoming me into the family.

To all my nieces, nephews, aunts, uncles, cousins, thank you for your love and support.

—*Lem Barney*

Contents

... ACKNOWLEDGEMENTS ...

To Gus Mollasis for the vision, tenacity, and love to undertake this arduous task of writing this autobiography of my journey through life. I will always be indebted to you. I would like to dedicate a special tribute to your dad who has gone to glory, thank you for your support, love, and encouragement and thank you for accepting me as one of the family.

To my friend, Del Reddy, who believed in this project from the beginning. His friendship with Gus Mollasis helped steer the book to Immortal Investments Publishing. Thank you to Publisher Mike Reddy of Immortal Investments for your attention to detail and for your genuine love, support, and concern you have shown to Jacci and me. We are forever grateful for your professionalism and your friendship that you and your wife Lorrie have shown us. Thank you to the entire team at Immortal Investments Publishing especially Jennifer Hilliker for her assistance and dedication to *The Supernatural.*

To all of the amazing editors—thank you for the long hours of labor, expertise, editing and writing skills you put into this book to make it the master piece it is!

To Dr. Bill Cosby for writing the Foreword as an expression of love. Thank you from the bottom of my heart; you are a wonderful friend and a great humanitarian. God bless!

To The Lion's Organization—Thanks in allowing me to be a part of a great organization and giving me an opportunity of a lifetime.

To all of my Coaches—college and NFL thank you for molding me into the athlete you knew I could be. Thank you for the discipline that I have carried with me through life.

To all of my former teammates thank you all for being my friend!

To my Hall of Fame Members, thank you for the friendship, camaraderie, and memories we share together. You are the greatest.

To my educators from middle school and college, thank you for the skills, knowledge, and concerns you shared with me.

To Chuck Colson with The Prison Ministry, thank you for allowing me the opportunity to speak in the prison ministry to inmates. Also, to Doctor James E. Moss, former Pastor of Springhill, thank you for bringing me into the ministry and may your soul forever rest in peace.

To my Pastor, Dr. Carlyle Fielding III and The Hope United Methodist Church—thank you for the Word of God. Thank you for your integrity, your dynamic preaching, and teaching and accepting Jacci and me into our new church home. Thank you for making us feel welcomed and loved

Lem Barney's story is filled with vivid descriptions of his athletic excellence on the gridiron. It is also the tale of a spiritual man who reaches out daily to the world and touches, hugs, and calms people with his inner peacefulness and charismatic personality. His current purpose is to dispel the warlike (i.e. violence, verbal admonitions, etc.) with which people are bombarded every day. His life is also about his own continuing transformation.

What is also beautiful about this athlete is that he was a genuine warrior on the football field who played with and against some of the most brutal and rugged men in any sport. He would mesmerize fans with his athletic wizardry and awe-inspiring maneuvers. Sometimes he would shift, shuffle, and accelerate in such a blur that it made you think that his helmet spun around his head and he was looking through the ear holes to intercept a pass.

Lem's transformation is possible because of what has been instilled into him through his loving and cohesive family. Barney's biological family provided him with sound answers to the problems in the world, and endowed him with the spiritual foundation necessary to navigate the trials and challenges that one faces during childhood and as an adult. His family provides that solid foundation and inner resource through which Lem continues to find and seek solace; moving forward while remaining positive.

At the age of 62, Lem's recollections of his mother and father's influence are still impacting him. He is able to recall the many familial interactions and lessons he learned and convey those in his story.

Lem's transformation continued after his hall of fame football career into a direction that was extremely difficult for him. He was gripped by the lure and intoxication of poison…drugs. During this period of negative evolution, Lem was simply a person who had once been successful in pro-football, but who was now on the precarious edge of despair. Ultimately, Lem was victorious. He faced this life threatening challenge and danger by his powerful and unwavering belief in God. Winners are those people who emerge alive and invigorated from personal adversity and then continue to "never fall into such a trap again."

Lem is a blend of a lot of different behaviors and characteristics. He is a gifted, inspiring soul who is as grounded as he is vibrant. He has not let religion dominate all aspects of his life, but it is the core that facilitates and guides him through this world. You will feel his engaging presence as I have while associating with him.

Lem continues his positive transformation daily while positively impacting each and every person he meets and embraces. He is a man of real spirit, not someone with the quick gift of gab who lacks genuine depth; his spirit is true. He is in control of his life and knows his future.

Lem Barney, who was magical on the field, is leading a life of excellence off the field as well. His transformation continues today as he has such a positive effect on people in his own inimitable way.

—Bill Cosby

If I magnify myself, I will accomplish ordinary things.
If I magnify God, He will use me in extraordinary ways.
I will be open to hear from God.

Learn God's plan
Make a humble commitment
Express my gratitude always
Express grateful praise

—Lem Barney—

✝ A PRAYER BEFORE WE START ✝

Our father who art in Heaven, hallowed be thy name, thy kingdom come, thy will be done—on earth as it is in Heaven.

Lord, we come before you with humble hearts and bowed heads to give you all the reverence, all the honor, all the glory, and all the praise. Lord, we love you, we adore you, and we worship your holy name. We thank you for allowing your only son to die on the cross at Calvary to save wretches like us—and all who believe. If we had ten thousand tongues, we could not praise you enough, but we love you.

We ask the Holy Spirit to fall fresh upon us to guide us in writing. Whatever is written, we want it to be for the edification and glorification of your holy name. Lord, we are empty vessels for you to fill and use. We want to tell of your greatness and the evidence of what you have done in our lives.

Lord, we pray that all who read this book will see the "Jesus" in it and that they, too, will give you all the praise and glory. Bless each reader and each person interviewed.

Bless our families and let your name resound in the writing of this book.

We pray this prayer in the mighty name of your darling son, Jesus Christ.

Amen.

—Lem Barney and Gus Mollasis

When I was a kid growing up in Detroit the 1960s, I didn't know the difference between living downtown or in the suburbs. I didn't care if a kid was short, tall, rich, poor, black or white. All that mattered was if he could play the game.

I knew the difference between a Piston and a Celtic, between a Red Wing and a Maple Leaf, between a Tiger and a Yankee, and between a Lion and a Viking. I could see and feel that difference as plain as the difference between night and day or right and wrong. In my mind, the Detroit Pistons, Detroit Red Wings, Detroit Tigers, and Detroit Lions were my good guys. Those other guys were the enemy—the bad guys.

Life back then was simple. You rooted for your team. Sometimes they won and sometimes they lost. But your job as a fan was to be loyal and pull for your heroes, no matter how bad the situation or the team may have looked.

Growing up with my heroes was one of the great joys of my life. I was enthralled listening to the Pistons, as Dave Bing and Bob Lanier performed their magic on the court. Watching legends like Gordie Howe and Alex Delvecchio skate down the ice at Olympia Stadium was a thrill I'll never forget. And sitting in Tiger Stadium watching Al Kaline, Norm Cash, Mickey Lolich, and Willie Horton—and later Alan Trammell and Lou Whitaker work their magic, made me feel blessed to be rooting for the Tigers.

But the biggest thrill of them all was watching my Detroit Lions marching down the field on Sunday afternoon, or during the traditional Thanksgiving Day game. I was always thankful for the Detroit Lions' good judgment in bringing to my town such heroes as Billy Sims, Barry Sanders, and the original Number 20, Lem Barney.

In them, I lived my youthful dreams. I always made the shot, caught the pass, scored the goal, or hit the ball out of the park. I could do no wrong, because in them I believed. They were special. They were great. And they were my heroes.

Like most kids, I really lived the old adage "Imitation is the sincerest form of flattery." So like the kid in the Bronx who copied

Babe Ruth or the kid on Chicago's south side who patterned himself after Michael Jordan, I too, imitated the heroes of my youth in Detroit.

I spent thousands of spring hours perfecting my Al Kaline stance, hundreds of winter days trying to shoot the puck like Mr. Hockey, Gordie Howe, endless summers trying to master my layup—à la Dave Bing—and finally so many brisk fall afternoons trying to intercept a football or run a punt back like Lem Barney.

In my youth, I was taught that if you're going to dream, dream big. And if you're going to try to be something, try to be the best. That was easy for me. In my youthful dreams, I was Howe in the winter, Bing in the spring, Kaline in the summer, and Barney in the fall.

During those seasons of my youth, I was very busy. Busy playing, but much more important, busy trying to be just like my heroes—trying to be the best.

As I got older, I had the great good fortune to meet each of these four men. I was honored to sit next to the great Gordie Howe at a hockey game, and I later did a book signing with him that ended with us walking to center ice, along with Mrs. Hockey, Colleen Howe. And all while my proud parents watched. Later, I met the incomparable Kaline at a golf tournament and was honored to join Dave Bing on the dais as we roasted our mutual friend Lem Barney.

Oh, how I remember them all, especially old Number 20—the original Lion King. And now, in one of life's interesting turns, I've gone from the pleasure of roasting my hero to becoming the author with the honor of toasting him.

Imagine that. I'm living every kid's dream. Getting to first meet, later befriend, and then tell others exactly just how great my hero is to the world. As Humphrey Bogart would've said, "It's the stuff that dreams are made of."

During lunch and gym class, I always wanted to cover the other team's best football player. I would get into coverage, and try my best to be just like No. 20. I would leave a little room for the receiver, then I would use my speed to close on the ball and pick it off. I had a little nickname for myself: The Interception King.

As I ran the ball back for a touchdown, I would yell out, "The Interception King!" As I raced across the goal line, I'd spike the ball and announce, "The Lions win another game on a beautiful touchdown by the great Lem Barney."

Even back then, I knew deep in my heart that there was only one "Interception King." He was so cool, so fast, and made it look so easy. Even more importantly, he played the game like he was having such fun out there. His legs churned, his body jittered. It was like watching Elvis Presley, James Brown, and Charlie Chaplin all rolled into one. He was so smooth, so graceful, and I wanted to be just like him.

Some years later, after yet another loss to the Minnesota Vikings, the phone rang. "It's for you," my dad said as he handed me the receiver.

"Hello, Gus. This is Lem Barney. How are you doing?"

I couldn't believe my ears. "I'm OK. How are you doing, Mr. Barney?"

"I'm OK, champ."

"Another tough loss," I said. "God, I hate those Vikings."

"Yeah another tough loss," Lem said. "But we'll be OK. We just have to keep playing better."

"Yeah," I said. "Just keep playing better."

"Keep playing better and keep praying better. I have to go, champ. Take care and God bless."

"Yeah, take care, Mr. Barney," I said as I hung up the phone.

My dad smiled at me.

"That was Lem Barney!" I said.

"I know, Gus," my dad replied. "I know."

The Lions had lost another game to the Vikings. But on the other side of town, some of my friends were getting together for a pickup football game. I had to go. There wasn't time to dwell on my sorrow after watching my guys lose. I was just a kid, and playing ball was something I was good at. There was still a little daylight left in a late fall Sunday afternoon, and a green field waited. My friends were on their way to our special place where passes would be thrown, interceptions made, footballs run back for touchdowns, and heroes imitated.

—*Gus Mollasis*

Make a joyful noise unto the Lord, all ye lands.
Serve the Lord with gladness,
Come before his presence with singing.
Know ye, that the Lord, He is God; it is He that hath made us,
And not we ourselves; we are his people and the sheep of
His pasture. Enter into his gates with thanksgiving, and into
His courts with praise: Be thankful unto Him, and bless His
name. For the Lord is good; his mercy is everlasting; and
His truth endureth to all generations.

—Psalms 100

The small black-and-white TV was tuned to the football game. The little boy from Mississippi, who would later become a star in his own right, studied the picture beamed into his home from a far away place called Detroit.

As young Lemuel Barney II watched the Thanksgiving Day game that had become part of the national holiday tradition, there was joy in his heart. He was thankful for many things—his parents, his sisters, food on the table, and that the TV worked. And that his Green Bay Packers were beating the Detroit Lions.

Little Lem Barney loved the Packers. There was something special about that team. As the game flickered on, he watched a Lions linebacker named Joe Schmidt make hard, solid tackles on his Packer heroes as they tried to fight their way out of the Green Bay backfield.

Snowflakes fluttered down, obscuring the helmets and jerseys of both teams. Shortly, the field became snow-covered and treacherous. This was a pleasant surprise for Lem. He'd never experienced snow, and the fascinating images of grown men slipping and sliding on the field were etched into his mind. As the snowflakes fell, so did the Lions and Packers. Little Lem grinned from ear to ear.

As he watched, he started to dream of that faraway place and the game being played there. In his mind, he was soon there—on that field of battle, sporting the green and gold of the Packers. He had become a star. He was making all the right moves, eluding Lions tacklers with ease. In the background, he could hear the play-by-play announcer calling the game:

"Barney has one man to beat. He makes a great move on the rookie linebacker and is at the 20, the 15, the 10, the 5 … touchdown! The Packers win the game on a brilliant play executed to perfection by the great Lem Barney from Gulfport, Mississippi.

In his mind, a voice of authority could be heard in the distance—someone commanding respect. But whose was it? It sounded like the voice of a stern football coach, but it wasn't the voice of Packers Coach Vince Lombardi. Whose voice was it?

The mysterious voice reverberated in his mind: "The Packers are going to have to play a perfect game to beat us. It's Thanksgiving Day in Detroit, and we are the Detroit Lions."

In a flash, young Lem Barney was able to put a name to the voice. It was the voice of Lions head coach Buddy Parker speaking to his team.

Interrupting this rapturous moment came his mother's voice: "Lem, you can watch the rest of the game after you finish dinner. And don't forget to say your prayers before you take a bite."

With those words from his loving mother, Lem's dream was over—for the moment.

"Thank you, Lord, for the gifts I am about to receive. Thank you for the plentiful food, and thank you for my family. And Lord, thank you for the Lions and the Packers," he prayed.

Lem remembers it all quite clearly. "I always watched the Lions on Thanksgiving," he says. "The Lions were the only thing I knew about Detroit. But it never occurred to me as a kid in Gulfport that someday I'd be playing in that game."

Lem says that during his eleven exciting years on the football field in Detroit from 1967 to 1977, Thanksgiving Day became a family affair—and he loved it dearly. "Playing on that day before much of the nation was very special," he says. "My family would often come from Gulfport to visit with me and to watch the game. The whole country was watching. And there was much to be thankful for. The team usually did well on Thanksgiving, and I was playing the game I loved with my family close by."

Lem's sisters Varina and Lemelda remember the excitement and warmth surrounding those unique Thanksgivings. "Lem would invite us to Detroit, and we would watch him play" Varina says. "Often, there would be snow on the ground, and that was a nice change of pace from our warm home state. These became special memories for all of us."

After those holiday games were over, Lem and his family would have their own Thanksgiving dinner. Lem was happy and he was thankful. He had played in the game that he loved—the same game that had intrigued him so much while watching on that small, flickering black-and-white television set back in Gulfport, Mississippi.

His dream had become a reality.

FOOTPRINTS

As scenes of his life flash before him, he noticed that there were two sets of footprints in the sand. He also noticed at the saddest and lowest times, there was but one set of footprints.

This bothered the man.

He asked the Lord, Did you not promise that if I gave my heart to You, that You'd be with me all the way? Then why were there but one set of footprints during my most troublesome times?

The Lord replied, My precious child, I love you and I would never forsake you. During those times of trial and suffering, when you see only one set of footprints, it was then that I carried you.

—Author Unknown

...Footprints II—The Little Boy...

Footprints were made in the sand. They were small footprints, but nevertheless, footprints all the same. And they were really the only evidence that he was, in fact, there at all on this late fall day. On the deserted beach, a gust of wind blew in the face of the lone inhabitant, as he struggled to maintain his footing in the sand. The soft white sand blew hard into his soft face, yet he continued on.

Running against the wind, the boy would repeat the ritual over and over. Once. Twice. A third time, followed by a fourth. And on and on until, mercifully, he ran out of breath.

Thank God he ran out of breath. He performed the feat twenty times and always for the same distance —100 yards and always against the wind.

There were no lines drawn in the sand. No markers to measure how far he had come or how far he had to go. He just knew. Knew that it was a long distance that he had to travel and that it would take him a long time to get there. So he continued on and kept running hard in one direction. The only direction that he felt would get him where he needed to go.

Sometimes he fell. But the little boy always got up. And many times, the sand that he kicked up sprayed directly into his face. Still he continued on alone—a small boy silhouetted against the reddening sky and pristine, white Mississippi beach. He was alone. Except for his doubts, fears, hopes, and dreams. They were always there to keep him company.

As he finished each sprint, he would talk to himself. Sometimes he really needed the encouragement.

"Come on, you can do it."

"You got it."

"You can get there."

Those were the voices that he liked to listen to in his head.

But other voices also appeared.

"Why do you think you're so special?"

"You *can't* do it."

"Give up."

The little boy could hear all the voices. And because of that, he sometimes slowed down. Yet he kept going. Kept moving in one direction. Kept running harder and faster toward the setting sun.

Soon, he could only hear one voice: The Holy Spirit. It was loud. It was clear. And he heard it with his heart.

"You *can* do it."

"You can do anything."

"You can be anything."

"You are my son."

Faster. Faster. Faster. Faster and harder he ran toward the sun and toward his goal.

"Just two more and I'll be done."

Almost out of breath, the little boy paused.

"Just one more, just one more," he said as he wheezed and gathered himself for one more run toward the sun.

"One more and I'll be finished. Just one more."

The little boy dug his frail legs into the white sand. His bare feet barely made an impression.

"Just 100 more yards and I'm done for the day."

He eyed his target. Then took off.

Tired from the previous 19 sprints, the little boy got off to a slow start. But in mid-stride, he found his rhythm. He eyed the goal. The prize and imaginary line was not drawn in the sand, but was carved into his heart.

"Just ten more yards to go," he said, as sand kicked up in every direction.

"Five more yards to go."

"Touchdown—I did it!"

Huffing and puffing, the little boy leaned over and paused for a moment of reflection as he looked into the glistening Mississippi sunset. But he would not rest long. He could not. He had to get home.

Still, the twelve-year-old boy had to sit for a minute and rest. As sweat poured out of him, he gasped for breath and waited for his wheezing to subside and his heart to stop pumping so fast. The rest was much-deserved and much-needed, and it helped him regain his strength. After all, he needed the newfound energy. The little boy still had a long way to go.

Before he got on his way, he paused and looked directly at the fading light and bright orange sun.

I can do this.

I must do this.

I will do this.

Then he took off running again. This time, toward home, homework, and a hot, home-cooked meal. The sun was setting on the beach. Night was approaching. The little boy did not like to run in the dark, so he picked up his pace a bit. In a few minutes, he was gone from the beach.

Strong winds kicked the sand up in every direction, and soon the little boy's footprints would be covered up. But the impression they made that day would last a lifetime. And the little boy who made them was now running home. Only now, little Lem Barney was running with the wind at his back.

In the Beginning

In the beginning was the Word, and the Word was with God and the Word was God.

—The Gospel According to John

HIS NAME WAS LEMUEL JACKSON BARNEY II, and he was good. Good to his parents, good to his siblings, good when he played and worked, but especially good when he prayed. Lem Barney was born in 1945 in the tiny Mississippi seaside town of Gulfport, to Lemuel C. and Berdell Barney. Their deep-rooted family ties remain in that area today.

Lem's grandfather was Barton Barney. Barton met his wife-to-be, Darina, in the Gulf Coast area after arriving in the south from his home in Cleveland. True to the Barney creed, Barton and Darina met in a good place—at a church function. They married shortly afterward, and ultimately, the family would consist of two sons and three daughters.

Life in the Gulf Coast area for young Lem Barney was part Tom Sawyer and part Huck Finn, with a bit of Porgy and Bess thrown in. It was a melting pot of experiences filled with crawfish, hammocks, and lots of love. "Summertime and the living is easy…catfish are jumping…"

Lem recalls a humble, love-filled upbringing. "My parents met in their early 20s, started courting, and later married," he says. "They were both caterers." Lem is their only son and the second in the birth order of three sisters, Rosemary, Lemelda, and Varina. While Lem may not have been rich in material things, he was wealthy in the commodities served at home—an abundance of love, humility, and faith.

Lem remembers some verses from the scriptures of King Lemuel that his mother taught him. "Growing up, they called me 'king' because of Proverbs 31," he says.

It is not for Kings, O Lemuel. It is not for kings to drink wine, nor for princes' strong drink...Open thy mouth for the dumb in the cause of all such are appointed to destruction...Open thy mouth, judge righteously, and plead the cause of the poor and the needy.

—Proverbs 31, Verses 4, 8, and 9

"I was literally treated like a king," Lem says. "I was spoiled good—not rotten—and my family domesticated me. I can still clean, cook, sew, wash, and iron. I'm clearly in touch with my feminine side. We were trained and taught to love one another. At our meals, we would recite: 'Let us live together and love one another.'"

Lem remembers his parents as two people who were affectionate toward each other. "My mom and dad had a great love affair," he says.

Evidence of that love was demonstrated almost daily by Lem's dad while he walked through the home softly singing, "Let me call you sweetheart... I'm in love with you" to his wife and life partner. They were perfect role models, singing together, dancing together, husband and wife, boyfriend and girlfriend. It was a great loving union.

Lem fondly remembers the advantages of being raised by two culinary master chefs. "They would cater country clubs, weddings and dances," he says. "Cajun food was their specialty."

In 1989, Lem's mom was diagnosed with a congenital heart condition and was admitted to Detroit's Sinai hospital for cardiac care. A pacemaker was ruled out after it was determined that it could not improve her condition. In her strength and wisdom, she simply said, "I will just take whatever the Lord gives me." Ten days later, she returned to Gulfport.

The last time Lem Barney would see his mom was in July of that year. His sister Varina lived with their parents and had told Lem that on the day before she died, their mother had a premonition that she would not be with them for her August 11th birthday. Varina felt that her mother's remark was only a passing comment. But that evening after going to bed, Varina grew concerned. Deciding to check on her mother, she arose and went to her parents' room, where she discovered that her mother's premonition had come true.

Lying peacefully next to her husband, who was unaware of her passing, Berdell Barney had gone to her glory. In shock and disbelief, Lemuel Sr. could not comprehend that his wife of over 50 years had left him. Without his spouse, he struggled and suffered.

Lem remembers with much sadness the hard times his father would go through trying to come to terms with the loss of his wife.

"He just couldn't believe it," Lem says. "He just didn't think he could make it without her, even with Varina taking over the daily household duties and taking care of him."

But Lemuel C. Barney's grief would not last long. A few months after his wife passed away, his daughter Varina returned home and discovered him kneeling next to Mrs. Barney's side of the bed, his hand gently positioned under his wife's old pillow. Only six months and one week after Berdell's passing, the voice that so often serenaded the family with the sweet strains of "Let Me Call You Sweetheart" followed her.

"Varina called me and gave me the sad news," Lem says. "Except for Dad's broken heart over the last few months, Mom and Dad left us without much suffering. I think if we all had a choice about the way in which we leave this earth, we would prefer to go the way they had. But we don't get to make that decision."

Lem reflects fondly on the lives of the two people who had the most profound impact on his life. "Mom had a great aptitude for teaching, while Dad was the disciplinarian," he says. "Mom's philosophy was to be serious about your work. One of her favorite phrases was 'Once a task has begun, never leave until it's done. Be it great, large, or small, do it well—or not at all.' Dad was also dedicated to 'do things right the first time and you won't be wrong.' He was a man who taught his children the importance of time and being on time. 'When you show up on time, you're late,' he would often say. 'Show up early—half an hour earlier than you were expected to be there.'"

While Lem Barney could count on his mother's kindness, he also realized that she meant business when it came to raising her children. "Mom was more compassionate than Dad," he says. "But if you did not do what you were told, you could expect to be punished by the loss of privileges."

The church also played a pivotal role with the Barneys, helping with the children's upbringing. In the Barney home, your faith was as vital as the food you ate. And to the Barneys, their faith was food for the soul.

"Attending church in our house was not an option," Lem says. "Saturday nights were devoted to preparing a proper outfit for the next morning's services. Dad did not want any last-minute stumbling around in the morning. In all we did, Mom and Dad taught us to be prepared—like Boy Scouts—for school, for church."

Lem's sisters Varina and Lemelda played key roles in the Barney household. "We were a great, loving Christian family," Lemelda says. "We all participated in school, and our parents were very supportive of us. When we couldn't find a ride to an event, they would get us a ride."

"We had a great childhood," Varina says. "Our sister Rosemary, who has since passed away, was 17 years older than Lem. She provided firm but loving guidance to the younger kids. We had a warm, close-knit upbringing, and we spent a lot of time together."

Together every Sunday, the Barney family headed to the Raleigh Chapel Methodist Church in Gulfport, where Pastor Haney resided over the pulpit. "He was a reverent man who had a tremendous love for the Lord and taught the Word," Lem says. "He was a great preacher and teacher."

Varina and Lemelda recall their church-going experience much the same way Lem does.

"We grew up learning that church and family were the most important parts of life," Varina says. "And we were taught that like the postman, neither, rain, sleet, nor anything else, should prevent our attendance in church."

But not everyone in Mississippi heeded the Lord's word. Lem remembers all too well dealing with the ugly issue of segregation. "Our culture was certainly different back then," he says. "There was not a lot of racial mixing, though it was not as bad on the Gulf Coast as other parts, due to the large military bases in the area. Interracial marriages had already been accepted, but there were still tensions because of desegregation. A small part of the beach on the Gulf Coast was earmarked as our regular spot for rallies and fish fries."

A warm, sentimental, almost melancholy feeling comes over Lem as he begins to paint a mental Norman Rockwell painting, framed by the memories of his youth. "It was a great area—palm trees, crab fishing…just a beautiful place," he says. "My Mom's dad, Jim Williams, was an expert fisherman. It was a joy to understand the geography and lay of the land out on the Gulf Coast, but it was not until I was in college that I truly understood the majesty of the gulf."

The foundation for Lem's great athletic talents was born and nurtured in Gulfport's sunny climate. "During the summer, it was sports from sun-up to sundown," he says. "Stickball, basketball, bicycling, softball, track and field, football, and fishing. It was a joy growing up, and I thought everybody grew up the way I did. It was only later that I realized not too many other kids received my training. I was a happy kid from a happy household."

Lem says athletics played a big part in his happy childhood, and he cherishes the friendships he made because of sports.

"I remember buddies like William Jones, Bobby Joe Jones, Robert Pryor, and John Thompson as I was growing up," he says. "Thompson was a great track-and-field star who played football and basketball. His style of play reminds me a lot of Barry Sanders. And I remember my cousin Elliot Barkum, who I tried to model my style of football after."

Other athletes who influenced young Lem were the Harlem Globetrotters. "In high school, I saw the Globetrotters with Goose Tatum and Marques Haynes," he says. "I had a chance to meet Meadowlark Lemon after a game. Herb Adderley of the Green Bay Packers was also a great role model for me. I was honored to play in the same division with his Packers."

Still, while growing up on the sandlots of Mississippi, Lem focused more on baseball than on football. From Manhattan to Montana to Mississippi, there was no better role model for kids—and surely no better ballplayer to imitate—than Willie Mays.

"When I was a young kid playing centerfield on the neighborhood baseball team, I once made a 'Willie Mays' catch," Lem says. "It was a catch just like Willie made in the 1954 World Series (off the bat of Cleveland's Vic Wertz). What a thrill."

Lem remembers having to overcome one very imposing—but very loving—obstacle: his mother. Berdell Barney stood between her son, Lem, and his dream of becoming a star athlete. "Since I was eight years old, I really wanted to be an athlete," he says. "But my mom was the principal obstacle. She'd heard of the many athletic injuries that occurred to other kids, and as a result, I was only allowed to participate in unorganized neighborhood sports.

"In school, she had me enrolled in the arts and sciences … the marching band…and I sang in the choir. I loved it all. It wasn't long before I had a whole set of drums and played in a group we called the Stardells. We had a great time playing in different clubs, at dances, and proms. It also provided me with spending money.

Lem's athletic side really came through in 1958. "My aunt Carrie Goods, who was living in San Bernardino, invited me to join her family in California and attend school there," he says. "Aunt Carrie had two kids of her own—a son who was two years older than me, and his sister. It was near the end of summer and I was in the eighth grade. My mom and dad approved of the idea. They bought me a Greyhound bus ticket, and I was on my way to California."

Lem remembers the one condition his mom attached to the trip. "I had to enroll in the band—and not play athletics at all," he says. "No athletics at all.

"It was the first time I had been away from home. My cousins lived there, and I just wanted to have an adventure and an exciting field trip." Lem credits this adventure as a major influence on his path to the NFL. "There was an area near their house with a big playground and a wide variety of sports being played there," he says. "It offered me my first chance to meet and mingle with people of different ethnic backgrounds and nationalities. It was there that I was first asked to play football."

Even at this young age, Lem turned the heads of all who watched. "I was able to make an impression on many of the kids there, and soon, a group of kids were asking me to play on their football team," he says. "But my eureka moment had not yet occurred."

Instead, he felt trepidation. "At home, I had been conditioned to be afraid of playing organized football. I declined their invitation and continued to play only in the unorganized sandlots. As time passed, a few parents of the local kids decided to visit my auntie to explain to her that I had the skills to succeed in organized ball." A week before school started, Lem's aunt finally consented. "But in doing so, she told me, 'If you get hurt playing football, your mother is going to kill both of us.'"

Due in part to his aunt's help, Lem had a phenomenal first season in which he narrowly missed being named Athlete of the Year at Sturgess Junior High School. Lem's biggest thrill that year was a 67-yard punt return for a touchdown.

"This was in 1958–59 in California and far away from Mom and Dad," Lem says. "Due to the distance that separated us, I wasn't able to communicate with my parents as often as I wanted. They didn't know about my California football career."

What Lem did know is that he liked California, and liked football even better because of what it taught him on and off the field. "I loved the weather and the people," he says. "I thought I had a chance to make more of myself and to meet many different types of people. I always enjoyed having the ability to play football and was convinced that my skills could match anybody's. But I was writing my mother often and was homesick. I made the decision to return home, to the dismay of all of my California friends."

Lem missed being with his parents and friends back in Gulfport. He had learned a new skill and looked forward to moving in a new direction. He was ready to head back home and try to apply his new knowledge there. He knew what to expect back home with the familiar sights, sounds, and smells of Gulfport. There was good food, an abundance of love, encouragement, and the compliments of a good mother who taught Lem who he was.

But Lem's mother said little about loving football. She preferred a music career for her son. As a result, when Lem returned home, he was enrolled at 33rd Avenue High School in Gulfport and was signed up to play in the band.

Football would be another story for another time. For now, the future Hall of Famer was not allowed to play the game he came to love so much. Obediently, Lem settled for the snare drum. As he played his drum and prayed for football, he asked God to lend a hand by using him as the instrument of whatever was in His will. And somewhere as Lem Barney prayed and played, he hoped that maybe, just maybe, he could change his mother's tune.

And the Band Played On

Seventy-six trombones led the big parade
With a hundred and ten cornets close at hand
They were followed by rows and rows
Of the finest virtuosos—
The cream of every famous band
—From "The Music Man," Meredith Willson

LEM BARNEY WAS AN ACTIVE AND competitive child. Whatever he tried, he was driven to master, either on the playing field, or in the marching band. As he entered the 10th grade, those two choices came crashing together like two cymbals.

"In the 10th grade I was in the school band and taking mandatory physical education classes," Lem recalls. "While playing flag football one day, the coaches were watching my footwork and passing ability. After class, they invited me to try out for the football team. The coach (Robert Hall) told me I had the necessary skills and potential. With my mother's opposition to my involvement in organized sports in mind, I went home and told my dad what the coach had said. My playing organized sports was not an issue with Dad, but as far as Mom was concerned, her mind was made up. While Dad listened to my pleas and agreed to check with Mama, a 'no' from her was not negotiable."

Still, Lem stayed with it and hoped and prayed to change his circumstances. "I continued doing things that I was expected to," he says. "A few weeks before the start of the football season, the coach approached me again and reminded me that the start of scheduled play was near, and again asked if I was going to join the team." When Lem told the coach that his mother still wouldn't allow him to play, the coach offered to come to the house and speak to her himself. In pursuing Lem, his future coach was displaying the same tenacity and resiliency that Lem would become known for on the football field.

Lem says that during his visit, the coach told his parents about their son's football potential and that there would be a very good chance that his skills on the field could earn him a college scholarship. But Lem's mother told the coach that she would prefer that Lem get a music scholarship and not risk serious injury.

The tenacious coach pressed on, trying to break the unbreakable mother, who also proved adept at playing a little defense where her son was concerned. "He has the skills, and I'll do anything if you'll allow him to come out and play with us," the coach said.

"You'll do anything?" Mrs. Barney repeated, with all the finesse and negotiating skills of a William Morris agent.

"Anything," the coach said. "I'll do anything you want."

The small woman of faith with a knack for gourmet cooking had the coach right where she wanted him. There was an idea simmering in that mind of hers. And while she had no briefcase, she had enough Southern charm and know-how to make her point. The coach never had a chance.

"I'll allow Lem to come out and play football," Mrs. Barney said, "if you'll allow him to play in the band at halftime."

Faster than Clark Kent can change into Superman, the coach shot back: "You have a deal!"

While no one in that small Mississippi kitchen knew it at the time, with that one little "yes" from a loving mother, Lem Barney was on his way to the NFL Hall of Fame.

Lem remembers it well. "At my first football game in high school, I was the only guy on the field at halftime playing the snare drum—in a football uniform," he says with a laugh.

This future hero of many Detroit Lions football fans would not only do his numbers on the field during the game, he would play a few of his own at halftime as he led the band. On both counts, he was a hit.

Lem's former high school band instructor, Dr. Willie Farmer, remembers a young man with an abundance of talent both on and off the field.

"I've known Lem Barney for more than 40 years," Farmer says. "I first met him in 1958 and have followed him from seventh grade all the way to the Detroit Lions. I knew he had the skills and dedication needed for success, and I treated him like another son. He was always delightful, and his mother was always there nearby.

"There are 24 to 26 fundamentals associated with drumming, and Lem Barney mastered them all. But I had to let him go from the band. I didn't want to hold him back."

But Lem did manage to participate in band after the season.

When Lem did get the chance to play in his first football game, he took full advantage of it. The top two quarterbacks on the depth chart had been injured, so Lem entered the game in the third quarter. Trailing by four points with two minutes left on the clock, Lem's team recovered a fumble deep in their own territory. With a minute and thirty seconds left, Lem called a few running plays and a couple of passes that got them out to their 20. "With 14 seconds left on the clock, Lem kept the ball on a quarterback sneak and ran for an 80-yard touchdown to win the game."

Lem's 33rd Avenue High School team was competitive, but not of championship caliber. "Our team was good, but we always came in second to Carver High in Mississippi," he says. "That team had beaten us in fifteen straight games and set a record. In the eleventh and twelfth grade when I was the quarterback, college scouts showed up in the stands during games."

It was the same coach who had to sell the idea of young Lem playing football to his mother, who also had to sell the idea of college to Lem. "Coach Hall wanted me to go to Jackson State University," Lem says. "He was from the city and had a strong influence on me. He was intelligent, a mathematician, and a no-nonsense kind of guy. Coach Hall would not play someone if he didn't believe they could get the job done."

Lem fondly remembers some of the players who were at his side and who the coach also believed in. "Some of those old teammates included Robert Tyler, who went on to play at Southern Illinois. There was Clive Frazier and Lawrence Peterson, who was a tremendous running back. Others were Henry Hallice, John Thompson, Elliot Barkum and Mel Friedman. Many had tragic deaths."

Others went to Vietnam and came back mentally scarred. "It was tough because a lot of them didn't have an interest in college. Some married early and had families to care for." But always watching out for Lem was his mother. "Mom wanted me to be an educator," Lem says. "My parents had spent a lifetime with hard work and long hours and didn't want me to go through the same thing."

Once again, the subject of football came up with Lem's mom. "I told my mom I thought I could make it as a ballplayer, and college scouts who read my newspaper clippings were coming to Friday night games," Lem says. "Naturally, I thought that was my door into college."

Jackson State would soon appear on Lem's radar screen, courtesy of coaches who cared. "John Meredith, the head football coach, and Harrison B. Wilson, the basketball coach at Jackson State University, and my coaches at 33rd Avenue High School, insisted that I go there," Lem says. "Coach Wilson attended one of the games I played. He told me I was unbelievable and said he was going to have the head football coach come down to take a look." And he did.

"Coach Meredith came with a letter of intent that I signed right away. This was the coach that had won the National Negro Championship. This was a great team at Jackson State University. I could see nothing but blue skies and clear highways."

Blue skies and clear highways that led a one-man band named Lem Barney to tiny Jackson State University.

Seventy-six trombones hit the counterpoint
While a hundred and ten cornets blazed away
To the rhythm of Harch! Harch! Harch!
All the kids began to march
And they're marching still right today!

Small Campus—Big Men

Photo by: Kirt Doke

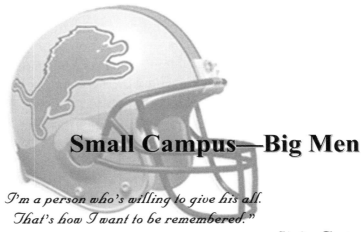

Small Campus—Big Men

I'm a person who's willing to give his all.
That's how I want to be remembered."

—*Walter Payton*

FOR SUCH A SMALL SCHOOL, "TINY Jackson State University," as Monday Night Football broadcaster Howard Cosell always emphatically called it, has produced three of the greatest football players ever to play the game — Walter Payton, Jackie Slater, and Lem Barney.

A big man on campus who played a big part in Lem's life, former Secretary of Education Dr. Rod Paige coached Lem when he roamed the sidelines at Jackson State. Paige theorizes why so many talented people came out of that small school and that small state of Mississippi.

"Mississippi produced Bob Johnson and Oprah Winfrey, so the state has had a reputation that was enthusiastic about achievement and moving ahead," Paige says. "Mississippi was slow in coming out of the early days of racial difficulties. The University of Mississippi did not move into black sports as quickly as Jackson State. Look at all the great ballplayers that went there: Lem, Payton, Slater, and Willie Richardson. Families grew up with great respect for Jackson State. Pride was so evident. It provided hope for me in terms of my educational foundation. Aside from my parents, Jackson State was the flame that burned inside me in terms of striving for my education."

Paige thinks of Lem as one of his greatest protégés. "He's a terrific guy," Paige says. "Lem is one of the finest athletes and finest people I have ever worked with. He came from a great family, and he's the kind of guy you enjoy coaching. In those days, we were disciplining athletes differently than we do now. It was clear back then that when you did something wrong, you needed discipline. Back then, an offending player would miss his meal in the dormitory and nobody wanted to miss a meal. Lem Barney never missed a meal."

Apparently, he never missed an assignment on the field, either. Paige remembers being taught a lesson by Lem. "We were playing Arkansas A&M, and I noticed Lem was off his man quite a distance," Paige recalls. "I preferred him closer to the guy. I said, 'Lem, you're too far off the guy.' Lem replied, 'But coach, I see the ball.' As I recall, I told him three times that he was playing too far off his man, and three times in that game he got damn interceptions. After that, I stopped giving him my advice."

Paige's new theory was simple. "Play it where you want to, Lem, just as long as you can see the ball," he told him.

Another man who goes way back with Lem is Joe Hoskins. Hoskins is known in Detroit sports circles as the winningest football coach in Detroit Public School history. But before his coaching career, he was just another green freshman with an eye for the football. And even then, Hoskins had an eye for talent.

"I'm a fellow Mississippian as well," Hoskins says. "I met Lem at Jackson State in 1963 when we were both freshmen. Lem played ball in Gulfport with a guy who had coached in my school by the name of Robert Hall. On the very first day, I think it was August of 1963, there was an unscheduled practice. I watched him walk across the street and there was just something about him. We became best friends and the rest is history." The two have remained friends for more than 42 years.

"He was special because he was a great athlete and a very kind person, and he had to be talented because he had played quarterback," Hoskins says. "In those days, you played both offense and defense.

Just watching him move—he had extreme grace. He had a very strong, unwavering will. Lem just believes that somehow or someway, it's going to get done."

Hoskins credits Lem's parents for concocting a perfect recipe for success. "I think it came from a combination of both his mom and dad," Hoskins says. "I know that spiritually, he's extremely strong—with an equally strong will. I cannot think of a time when Lem doubted himself at all. After our first year, we put a team together and challenged the Jackson State basketball team—and beat them. I was not surprised.

In Lem's first season, Jackson State opened against Grambling and Otis Taylor, a fellow Hall of Famer who later played for the Kansas City Chiefs. "There were times when Lem would do remarkable things on the field," Hoskins says. "I initially thought he was maybe just lucky. But I soon realized that luck had little to do with his success. Lem really did have supernatural talent."

Lem counts his blessings and is thankful for the friendship he forged with Hoskins. "Those many years ago, Joe and I walked the campus at Jackson State together, and he remains one of my oldest and dearest friends," Lem says. "He is an upright brother who loves people and has done well through that philosophy." The two reunited in 1967 when Hoskins came to Detroit after he'd been cut by the San Francisco 49ers.

Hoskins remembers Lem for his giving nature. "While coaching high school in Detroit, every time I asked Lem to talk to my players, he would be there," Hoskins says. And to further enhance the experience for Hoskins' kids, Lem would bring along teammate Mel Farr and Detroit Pistons star Dave Bing, who would also talk to the players. They would counsel the youngsters on the ingredients necessary for a player to make it to the pros, as well as in life.

"One year, five of my players moved up to the pros," Hoskins says. "I feel that those talks from Lem and the others of his caliber played a great part in the ultimate success of my kids. It was truly inspiring to have players who had been so successful take time to come back and speak directly to you. That was Lem Barney. I'll never forget it. And I'm sure those kids did not forget either."

Lem remembers the day the Detroit Lions first caught a glimpse of him. "Chuck Knox and Lou Creekmur came down to Jackson State to watch me play," he says. "After the NFL draft, [Dick] Night Train Lane and Will Robinson also came down on a scouting trip."

"When Creekmur came to scout me at Jackson State, he was the only white guy in the stadium," Lem says. "We still laugh about that."

"I'm the guy that drafted Lem Barney," Creekmur says, "and I was the only white guy in the stadium that day. [Lions General Manager] Russ Thomas sent me there to scout Lem and to see if he was an appropriate draft pick." It wasn't long before Creekmur had his answer. "From the minute the ball was snapped and until the whistle was blown, Lem was giving 300 percent," Creekmur says. "That's what a professional scout is looking for in a potential pro football player—a guy that doesn't give up on a play. Lem's dedication and commitment are the reasons he was as good a defensive halfback as has ever played the game."

Joe Schmidt, Lem's head coach for his first six years in the pros, isn't sure how his prized rookie was discovered. "I can't recall exactly how it happened," Schmidt says. "But when word gets around about someone capable of doing the things that a Lem Barney does, everybody wants a little credit for discovering his kind of talent." Holding to the old saying, "Failure is an orphan and success has many fathers," Lem Barney's success story has many fathers, mothers, sisters, and brothers.

Fellow Southwest Athletic Conference great Mel Blount echoes those beliefs. "I went to Southern University, and Lem went to Jackson State, he says. "Those two black colleges have produced some outstanding talent for the NFL. And Lem, the tremendous player, was one of them."

Lem also recalls fellow Jackson State alumnus and former Chicago Bears great Walter Payton. He was a big man from a small campus who exemplified the kind of grit and grace that Lem has always looked up to in a man. Payton's nickname, "Sweetness," described his character and play both on and off the field. "I played three years against Sweetness as NFC Central division rivals," Lem says. "We were friends and he came into the league nine years after I did. He came out of college as a number one draft pick. But since Jackson State was a Division II school, Payton didn't get a true shot at the Heisman Trophy, as he should have." But later, Payton helped solidify the Chicago Bears and turned the team around, leading them to a Super Bowl in 1986.

Lem remembers what made this man from his alma mater so special. "You can look at guys and tell if they possess those special gifts for running or avoiding big hits," he says. "That natural talent cannot be taught. Payton had avoidability and escapability, but he also had the tenacity to run right into a pile or a defensive end. It didn't matter. He had a fearless attitude." If Payton was thrown for a loss on one play, he would be up and ready to go by the next. "He was a very special ballplayer," Lem says. "We knew that from his junior year at Jackson State, when he was a Heisman candidate. I was honored to call him my friend. Walter Payton had grace and courage both on the football field and in the field of life. He was one of the finest running backs I've ever played against."

Lem also admires another Bears Hall of Famer, Gale Sayers. "Sayers was always a tremendous competitive threat," Lem says. "But because he left the game so early in his career, I only had the opportunity to play against him for five years. Sayers would use his remarkable speed to avoid as much heavy contact as possible. Walter shared Sayers' gifts, but wasn't as shifty."

Rookie

When you're green, you're growing.
—McDonald's founder Ray Kroc

THE PHONE RANG IN THE DORM ROOM AT Jackson State. On the other end of the line was Lem Barney's mother. On that day in 1967 when the NFL held its draft to choose from the brightest talent in college football, the young man from the sleepy town of Gulfport, Mississippi, went about his business as usual. But soon, his thoughts would turn to visions of Lions, Supremes, and Fords.

"I was in the dormitory during the draft after working on drills with a group of seniors," Lem says. "After we finished a late brunch, I took a nap. A little later, someone yelled through my door that there was a long-distance phone call for me. It was my mother. She told me she heard some news on the radio." With that, the slender young man sprang to his feet the way a Marine does when his drill sergeant enters his barracks without warning.

"What did they say, Mom?"

"Lem, I just heard the news on the radio—the Detroit Lions picked you!" she said.

"A Detroit Lion," he thought to himself. "A Detroit Lion." The newest Lion was familiar with the team that he'd watched on Thanksgiving Day in the annual game against teams like his favorite club as a child, the Green Bay Packers.

Still, with a bright future and a brand-new bachelor of science degree, Lem was surprised. "Back then," Lem says, "both the Giants and 49ers were scouting me. They had both expressed interest, and I thought for sure that it would be either New York or San Francisco calling. But that wasn't meant to be. It seemed that I was meant to be a Lion. But my surprise did not dampen my excitement at having been drafted into the NFL and to be heading to Detroit."

Lem wasn't intimidated by the move to Detroit. He felt that if the good Lord wanted him to play there, then that's where he was going to play. "All I knew about the Lions was that I had been drafted into the great Thanksgiving Day game. I knew nothing about the city, other than automobiles were made there, and it was the home of the famous Motown sound."

The Motown sound was truly music to Lem's ears. The idea of playing in Detroit with all that tradition sounded good to him. "It didn't take long before I felt right at home in Motown," he says. "I went to work learning more about the place where I would be working, playing, and praying."

Soon, Lem would be off to his first NFL training camp. He was excited, young, and green. But he was definitely growing. As he took the field at Cranbrook Institute for his first practice, the Lions' higher-ups didn't know what to expect from their second-round draft pick. They knew what the team needed, though—someone with the skills to fill the incredible hole created by the departure of the legendary Dick "Night Train" Lane.

"I was a 21-year-old rookie who had just graduated from Jackson State University," Lem says. "I came to training camp and it was a joy; it was the realization of my dream." But for the Lions management, they knew their collective reputation was on the line, after making Lem their number two draft pick.

"Three weeks after signing with the Lions, I was to graduate," Lem says. "A week before graduation, I received a brown manila envelope from the military. The letter stated that I would be inducted into the military following graduation, since my Selective Service status would be changed due to the loss of my educational deferment. After advising [Lions general manager] Russ Thomas of this situation, I learned of another option for fulfilling my military obligation that would give me the chance to continue in professional football—a 36-month commitment for service in the Naval Reserves."

For Lem, fulfilling his dream of becoming a professional football player was his number one priority. "I loved practicing because I knew that practice was the only way to learn, improve, and prepare for the game," he says. "It was my approach to study game plans, watch film, and execute in practice. In doing so I was building my confidence."

Players often talk of how important practice is, but until they actually do it right, it doesn't become a part of them. "While in the league," Lem says, "I cultivated the friendship of other players who shared my spirit for practice. One of them was Mike Weger." Lem and Weger were rookies together. They both loved singing and reading the Bible. "We played side by side," Lem says. "The team had a game plan, and Weger and I had one, too. We made it a rule to always have fun in practice." Lem found out later that because he and Weger had so much fun playing and didn't seem to feel the pressure the others did, many of the veterans thought they had no-cut contracts.

"I had no trepidation about going into the Lions locker room and had great respect for the veterans. But I knew that having been a member of Alpha Kappa Phi, that I was sure to be hazed." Since singing to the team was one of the main hazing techniques, Lem actually looked forward to it. "Singing was my forte," he says. "By tradition, rookies were required to stand up in front of the team and sing. And Mike and I were ready to do it. We would be required to entertain our teammates with each other's college songs."

Lem's teammates, as well as Lions management, certainly enjoyed the tune the rookie was singing—good practice habits, great ability, and outstanding attitude. It was all coming together in the early days of training camp for both the Lions and Lem. They were getting into game-day shape, but neither was 100 percent of what they would become. Like two lovers in the early stages of dating, each getting to know the other and discovering what they could and could not do, the Lions management was watching to see what their new cub could do. And the cub was looking to management for direction.

Within professional football, there are always doubts about the abilities of newly drafted rookies. And there were doubts about how good Lem would be, including those in the mind of head coach Joe Schmidt. Schmidt had reluctantly agreed to draft Lem, based on the strong recommendations of Night Train Lane and Will Robinson, who both witnessed Lem's exploits at Jackson State.

Schmidt watched Lem with an objective, but cynical eye of a general planning his next battle. All he saw when he first looked at Lem was a green rookie. At an early preseason press conference, Schmidt was asked if Lem would see much play in his rookie year. "Pretty damn little," Schmidt replied. "It takes longer to learn how to play cornerback in this league than almost any other position." As Lem's training camp experience rolled on, skeptics appeared in droves, writing stories, forming their opinions, and observing first-hand the play of a rookie who hoped he could make all of them forget about a man named Night Train.

Some members of the press spared Lem the unfair comparisons to the legendary Lane. After all, Night Train had rewritten the job description for a Lions cornerback. But now the Train had left the station. It was time for a young Lion to show the organization just what he could do. Lions defensive coach Jimmy David, an outstanding safety with Detroit's championship teams of the 1950s, also wanted to see what Lem brought to the table.

In one of their early training-camp workouts, David wanted to test Lem, so he matched him up with former All-Pro receiver Gail Cogdill. A first pass was thrown in the Cogdill's direction. Lem deflected it without flare and without much effort. The two men, one a former All-Pro, and the other a hopeful rookie, returned to their respective huddles. On the next play, they lined up across from each other, both with something to prove to themselves and the coaching staff. For the old pro, perhaps that he still had it. For the rookie, perhaps merely that he belonged.

On the second play of Lem's first professional training camp, quarterback Karl Sweetan went back to pass in the direction of Lem and Cogdill. Reading the play like a veteran, Lem leaped around Cogdill and made a brilliant one-armed interception.

"That was pass interference!" Cogdill screamed.

Without missing a beat, Lem smiled and asked, "Did you mean offensive or defensive interference?" Everyone in attendance still remembers that play.

Veteran DETROIT NEWS sportswriter Jerry Green was there. "People were wondering who Lem was because the first guy they took in the draft was [UCLA running back] Mel Farr, and he was quite well-known," Green says. "I got my first impression of Lem on the field during that scrimmage when he made that play against Cogdill. Cogdill was, after all, one of the best receivers in the NFL at the time. But Lem didn't care about Cogdill's stats. All he said after the play was, 'Offensive or defensive?' I knew right then that Detroit was going to have a very colorful and dynamic player for us to cover in the press."

As Lem returned to the huddle following his interception, hope sprang eternal in his heart. On this day in training camp, the memory of Night Train Lane had already begun to fade. On the sidelines, a battle-scarred general named Schmidt jotted down a note on his clipboard. He may have even smiled a bit as he evaluated his number two draft pick.

1967: A Year of Rookies, Riots and Rewards

The world is black, the world is white
It turns by day and then by night
A child is black, a child is white
Together they grow to see the light, to see the light
—Black and White
David Arkin & Earl Robinson

*D*ETROIT IN 1967 MEANT JUST ONE THING: The Riots. It was the story on the streets of Detroit and across the nation. The front pages of newspapers and evening newscasts, replete with all the brutal images, were focused on the city. Detroit was, at that moment, a people and a place gone wrong. Forever, those images of upheaval and tension between the races, the decay of a once-proud city, would label Detroit with the stereotype that to many, it still holds today. A tough city, a dangerous city where blacks and whites don't get along.

Detroit was no longer the place where they made great cars, made great sacrifices for a war, or made great music. Detroit was now a place where chaos reigned, where there was mob rule and where the dancing in the streets had come to an abrupt halt. In its place were bloodshed and broken windows, gunshots and fires, beatings and broken dreams. To many, Detroit was a war zone. For Lem, this would be his new home. It must've seemed like a million miles from Gulfport.

"During my rookie year, I stayed downtown at the Leland House on Bagley," Lem says. "At that time, Detroit was a warmly welcoming place—literally." The city was on fire and in the throes of a riot. Since first coming to Detroit and now as a proud resident of the area, Lem recalls that he had served on many civic boards and committees over the years charged with working toward bringing the city back to its previous glory.

But back then, in the heat of the summer of riots, Detroit was in no way ready for any renaissance. Lem looked at his situation in the only way he knew how—with a straightforward attitude that tries to make the best of a difficult situation.

"There was civil unrest around the country," he says. "There had been a campus riot at Jackson State and at Kent State as well. Neil Young wrote a song about it—but nothing like this. I was driving to Detroit during the week of the riot. That was an eerie feeling, not knowing what was actually happening. I was just coming up for a job."

In reflecting on his experiences during the riots, Lem recalls a man he idolized—a man who devoted his life to improving race relations. "Dr. Martin Luther King was a renaissance man with a great calling," Lem says. "He was called to bring forth to the masses the issues of social injustice—and to provide hope. Growing up, I witnessed many injustices. I remember the Emmitt Till matter in upper Mississippi. Emmitt had lived in Chicago earlier and had returned home to Mississippi. It was alleged that he had whistled at a white woman. For that offense, he was beaten, hung, and his body thrown into the river."

For the most part, Lem remembers a world far from this type of violence. "When I was growing up, we weren't taught to hate," he says. "My mom and dad taught their kids that evil does not arise from good, and only God has the moral authority to practice 'an eye for an eye.' Because of my upbringing, I've always viewed people as just people and to try to do unto others as I would have done unto me. And the words of Dr. King have always guided me."

Martin Luther King provided hope for all oppressed minorities, not just African-Americans. His greatest legacy was bringing an awareness of existing social problems to all people, by introducing those who had more to those who had less, and by showing people that there is still oppression in the world that needs to be addressed. His greatest quote was that he hoped his four children would be judged not by the color of their skin, but by the content of their character.

"Dr. King died in 1968 after my first season with the Lions. It was a remarkable and devastating experience for me and the country. The night he died, I had visited the Lindell AC's owners, Jimmy and Johnny Butsicaris. While there, news arrived of King's death. We sat in silence in front of the restaurant's television and tried to comprehend how and why something like this could have happened, especially to a man who had devoted his life to the non-violent resolution of racial problems."

While they sat there, the three men felt a growing concern that Dr. King's death could lead to more turmoil like the riots of 1967. "In my mind, I sensed a growing fear creeping across the city that could lead to great unrest. For the next eight hours, I found myself confined to the Lindell AC. The city had just come to a stop. Everything was shut down. You couldn't go anywhere."

Reflecting on King's assassination, Lem spoke for decent people everywhere. "Everyone who supports justice and fairness was touched by Dr. King's loss," he said. "Dr. King represented not only the moral quest for justice, but he also represented one part of a trilogy of honor—Dr. King, John F. Kennedy, and Robert Kennedy. In speaking with my teammates, I learned that the desire for peace and honor crosses all racial, religious, and ethnic lines. But even today, it seems that nothing has been finalized. Dr. King's death was a dagger in the heart of all reasonable people."

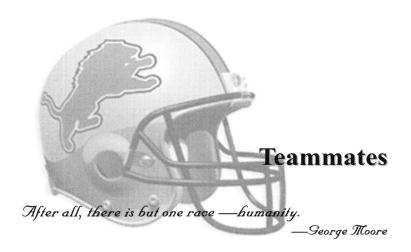

Teammates

After all, there is but one race —humanity.
—George Moore

$\mathcal{I}$N DETROIT, THE GREAT MARTIN LUTHER King challenge would be placed directly on the shoulders of two rookies— Mike Weger and Lem Barney. These two played together with extreme closeness both on and off the field. The Lions had decided they would be roommates. In football, like perhaps no other game, the guys you suit up with are the guys you "go to war" with. Teammates rely on each other to do their jobs so they can live to fight another day. It's this camaraderie and feeling of brotherhood that football players miss most after leaving the game.

Lem defined his career by being there for all his teammates, and they were there for him. It's an unwritten code. Teammates share the good times and bad, the spoils of victory and the bitterness of defeat, the hilarity of hazing rookies and the unspeakable sorrow of watching a teammate die on the field.

"Our friendship as rookies was priceless," Weger says. "He was a black kid from Gulfport, Mississippi, and I was a white kid from Durant, Oklahoma. Both our hometowns had populations of less than 9,000 people." It was their mutual love of music that brought the unlikely pair closer together.

"I grew up listening to all kinds of music," Weger says. "My father was a music professor, and I remember listening to black radio from Nashville. Back in the 1950s, I knew a lot of black music that most white people had never heard of."

Lem didn't know much about Weger when they arrived at camp, but something in him soon struck a chord. "Whenever I heard a phrase from a song I knew," Weger says, "I would start singing. Most everyone I came to the NFL with didn't recognize most of those tunes, but Lem knew them all... After awhile, we would start harmonizing in the middle of practice to songs that no one else knew, and that created an incredible bond."

If music was one element that bonded their relationship, their work ethic solidified it. "From the minute we came to training camp, the two of us were sprinting out in front of all the defensive backs," Weger says. "Players normally come into camp to get into condition, but we were already in good condition. [Coach] Jimmy David had us doing sprints and gassers. Lem and I would bolt out in front. We would be halfway across the field well before the rest of the veterans. I remember on one of the first days, one of the old veterans yelled out at us, 'You [bleeping] rookies … you think you're going to make this team because of sprints? Slow down.'"

"If [the coaches] said, 'sprint,' Lem and I sprinted. The veterans hated both of us."

Weger remembers veteran Roger Shoals expressing his disdain for them and their work ethic. "We were having a beer in a casual setting, and Shoals confronted us. 'I hate you rookies coming in with no-cut contracts,' he said. 'You make the rest of us look bad.'"

Weger politely told Shoals that they didn't have no-cut contracts.

"Why do you think we have no-cut contracts?" Weger asked him.

"You two are always so happy—singing and having a good time. Practice isn't stressful for you."

Weger laughs at the memory. "It was just our nature," he says. "We came into camp in good shape, and the reason we were singing was simply because we're happy people." And they clearly loved what they were doing. "Getting paid for having so much fun was like stealing," Weger says.

An NFL tradition of hazing rookies by making them sing barely phased Lem and Weger. In fact, they relished it. "When they asked us to get up and sing, we belted it out," Weger says. "We'd get applause from the veterans. Half the time, I would sing Lem's alma mater's song, and he would sing mine. Jackson State... Gee, I love my old college home…"

Weger and Lem played together, sang together, and prayed together. And they did something that was unheard of back in the day. "We were the first white and black guys in the NFL who requested to room together on the road," Weger says. "It was strained times in general in the whole United States. But I don't remember it being an issue with any teammates. I don't recall even one player or coach asking, 'What do you think you guys are doing?' Lem and I were so focused on playing ball, and we had so much fun together."

Weger remembers how race could affect a team's roster, too.

"Management was always looking for ways to save money," he says. As a result, if the team had an odd number of black players going on a road trip, one would be cut before the trip. Had they not done so, it would have been necessary for a white and a black player to room together. That was before Lem and Weger asked to room together, which changed the whole situation. "[Lions running back] Tommy Watkins told Lem and me, 'You guys have no idea what you did in terms of relationships in the NFL,'" Weger says.

In setting standards on the field, in the locker room or on the road, Lem and Weger formed quite a pair. "We came to camp with milk on our breath," Weger says. "We were very naive. After practice, we would go to a place called Ted's on Woodward. Lem and I would order ice cream sundaes while the other guys were having beers."

This style permeated every aspect of their lives. "We had a wholesome attitude toward living that resulted from our upbringing," Weger says. "And it was our attitude toward Christ, toward living, and toward human relationships. The respect automatically developed between us—both off the field and on."

Lem and Mike made their bread and butter by sticking as close as they could to the receiver while watching each other's front and backside. "Lem, Paul Naumoff, and I were on the left side," Weger says. "Every break in the team huddle, Lem and I would have our own mini-huddle. We would repeat the defensive play to ensure that we didn't make a mistake. It was that kind of camaraderie that just came from living your lifestyle, religion, and attitude on the field. It manifested itself in that matter of respect for people and the effort that you're giving."

The Lions' left-side trio formed a defensive alliance that was all but impossible to penetrate. "We used to call it the Bermuda Triangle," Weger says. "Lem, Paul Naumoff, and me. If you came into our area, you weren't coming out." Lions' opponents were well aware of this, and avoided throwing into the Triangle whenever possible. "We did everything we could to put the team in a position to win," Weger says. "We were both incensed at losing. I remember after we had lost yet another game to the Vikings, Jimmy David told me that I had played a nearly perfect game. I didn't care. I looked at him and said, 'But we lost, Jimmy.'"

One thing that's not lost is the respect and admiration that Weger feels to this day about his old teammate. "Our professional and personal relationship was priceless," he says. "We didn't know what was going to happen in the NFL, but we had an ability to bond, have fun, and make a mockery of what everyone else thought was drudgery." All the while, Lem and Weger displayed a stronger work ethic than most. "Our focus was absolute," Weger says. And the results speak for themselves.

Mel and Lem

"You and me will be the greatest partners, buddies, and pals."
—*Jerry Lewis and Dean Martin, "Partners"*

MEL FARR FROM UCLA, LEM BARNEY from Jackson State. They came into the NFL together as the Lions' No. 1 and No. 2 picks in the 1967 draft. For the most part, the two have stayed together as friends. And as rookies, they almost turned this franchise around.

While their pedigrees were different, their performance on the field was similar, especially in that first year. Together, No. 24 Farr and No. 20 Barney dazzled the league with their talents. They were very close, Lem says. And the Detroit media had a field day with the on-field exploits of the two star rookies.

A natural public relations campaign ensued:

Lem is Mel backward.

Mel is Lem forward!

"We had a lot of fun with it," Lem says. "I never had a brother growing up, and Mel was like that brother to me. We roomed together for five years in the league. In each other, we recognized dreams coming true. Mel is a tremendous, hard-working guy and has become one of my best friends."

It was the beginning of a beautiful friendship. "We've been very close since that day at the press conference when we first met," Farr says. "Lem is the kind of guy that radiates charisma and he makes you feel you've known him forever. He's cheerful, polite, and has a great gift of gab—and loves to give out love."

Farr remembers when he first noticed Lem—at the College All-Star Game, which pitted the best college players against the reigning NFL champs. The All-Stars were battling the Green Bay Packers, the team Lem idolized as a youngster. And even though the college players lost 27–0, Farr was impressed. "It was Lem's first game [against the pros], and he played like a bullfighter," Farr says. "He would just go around guys and make tackles. He had the most unbelievable quickness, agility, and athletic ability that I had ever seen."

Not only did Lem play tenacious defense, but he ran back kicks and punts—and punted. "His natural ability was remarkable," Farr says. "He was so good I think he could play in today's league. Most people would die to have a cornerback like him."

Coach

*"A teacher affects eternity;
he can never tell where his influence stops."*
—Henry Adams

𝓗E WAS MORE THAN JUST THE LEADER with a clipboard, more than just the man wearing a headset who called the plays, and definitely more than just Lem's boss. To Lem, the coach was the leader you trusted. The person you counted on to keep things calm when the storms on the football field approached, and the outcome of a game was on the line. While everyone else was losing his head or his headset, it was the coach's job to remain cool.

To Lem, Joe Schmidt was more than just a coach. He was man who commanded respect and a man who should be respected both on and off the field. Schmidt's pedigree demanded respect. He had played on the Lions championship teams of the 1950s. He was a great defensive player. And he was the one whose opinion would determine how much Lem would play during his rookie year.

Lem knew and respected the coach's judgment and authority. In his mind, he hoped the coach would see his greatness while being scrutinized under that watchful eye. And the coach hoped—and maybe even prayed—that he would find that greatness in Lem.

Schmidt was a coach, a friend, a teacher, and a father figure. Lem was a player, a friend, a student, and like a son. That's how history would define their relationship. In some aspects, the coach and the player may have a relationship similar to that of a father and son. A son asks the father for the keys to his car. The father hopes that he can trust the kid with all that responsibility.

"Coach Schmidt took over the head coaching job with the Lions in 1967, and was like a father to me," Lem says. Mike Weger, Mel Farr, Nick Eddy, Paul Naumoff, Frank Gallagher, and Lem made up the Lions' crop of rookies that year. "In his first speech to us, Coach Schmidt said, 'Give me the best you have and we're going to have fun.'"

From that day on, Joe Schmidt earned Lem's admiration. "I have all the respect in the world for him," Lem says. "He taught his players to be true to themselves on and off the field. Always be upfront with people and know your strengths and weakness. Know the things that you need to work on. Your work ethic is what you'll be rewarded for. And have fun with what you're doing."

Schmidt did not play favorites. He loved all his ballplayers equally because he was one himself.

"Things don't always work out the way we would want," Lem says. "The biggest problem Coach Schmidt had with the team's management was related to his desire to remain involved in the draft. When that responsibility was denied him, he took it personally and decided to retire."

Lem still fondly remembers the man who was more than just a coach to him. "To this day, Coach Schmidt and I have maintained a close friendship and speak to one another regularly on the telephone," he says. "He's a great guy and he played the game with such tenacity, he was ultimately inducted into the NFL Hall of Fame."

Schmidt recalls the once-green Jackson State prospect who blossomed into a Hall of Famer himself. "We never fully established who in the organization discovered Lem," Schmidt says. "I really cannot tell you who first watched Lem play. But as soon as he arrived and put on the Lions colors and walked onto the field, he looked like a natural. I would tell him what to do and he would do it. He understood our game from the beginning."

From the first time he saw his prize rookie cornerback in person, Schmidt had no doubt he would make the team. "He had great speed, intuitiveness, and a great feeling of what needed to be done and what the other guy was most likely going to do," he says. "Lem had great closing speed to the ball and to the receiver, and his practice habits were excellent. He played hard and was the kind of guy who was very happy being on a football field. He really loved football and was a team leader for us."

When Schmidt left Detroit, it seemed that the Lions could not get back on track. A revolving door of coaches ensued. Myriad questionable personnel decisions left the once-proud franchise in disarray. The decline left one All-Pro cornerback scratching his head.

Schmidt is emphatic in his belief that the attributes Lem brought to the field in the 1960s and 1970s would make him a star in today's game. "Are you kidding me?" Schmidt says. "He could play in any era. These guys could not hold a candle to him. He's a great athlete with a great mix of skills. I cannot describe it. He's probably one of the best athletes we have ever had in Detroit. He is a guy you could count on all the time. He had confidence, and his teammates and I had confidence in him."

Schmidt goes so far as to say he'd like his sons to be just like Lem. "My son Billy was 12 years old at that time, and Lem gave him a pair of his shoes from training camp. Kids were always hanging around Lem, and I knew he had a love for his fellow man and for the game. He always had a good time and was very positive. His attitude lit a fire under everyone."

A fire that burns to this day in the hearts of a player and coach and of a father and son.

"Lord, Is *This* Going to Be Easy"

*"Do not be too timid and squeamish about your actions.
All life is an experience."*

—*Ralph Waldo Emerson*

THE JITTERY ROOKIE DANCED ONTO THE green grass of Lambeau Field accompanied only by the butterflies in his stomach. He had arrived. He was finally here at the place that he'd dreamed about ever since he was a little boy on the sandy beaches of Gulfport, Mississippi. And he was about to start his first game in the National Football League. Soon, he would show his detractors just why the Detroit Lions chose him with their second pick in the draft.

The young man from the sleepy Gulf Coast town was playing on the hallowed grounds of the Green Bay Packers. Just saying those words sent the adrenaline surging through Lem's veins. If he did have a few butterflies in his stomach, they were probably green and gold. All he ever wanted to be was a professional football player. And now he was. At this time and in this of all places, the rookie with the slick moves and nervous energy was about to make his debut. "It was a dream come true," he says.

Glaring from the opposite side of the field was a man whose profile was more suited for Mount Rushmore than for the sidelines. "Vince Lombardi was larger than life," Lem says. "He was a great coach and an even greater man. I had the utmost respect for him and the Green Bay Packers and all that they'd come to stand for."

What they stood for went beyond success, beyond Lombardi's famous dictum:

"Winning isn't everything; it's the only thing."

Winning, to the Packers, was just as much about how you played the game, as it was in the final score. "They always played with class and dignity," Lem says. "They had reverence and respect for the traditions and contributions of those who had come before. That respect for the game was instilled directly into his players by one man—coach Vince Lombardi."

Growing up, Lem was a Green Bay fan. "I loved the Packers," he says. "They were my favorite team throughout high school and college. But above all, I respected that organization and its rich history."

History or not, the rookie from tiny Jackson State was about to set aside his great respect for the Packers and hold his green-and-gold butterflies in check, as he stepped onto the field of his football dreams.

The Lions kicked off and the Packers downed the ball for a touchback, starting their opening drive on their 20-yard line. No time had elapsed on the clock. The rookie Lions cornerback wearing No. 20 took the field.

Lem was so excited, he was downright jittery. "But my good luck, training, and confidence led me to believe that I was indestructible," he says. "As a child, I thought I could be shot by a cannon and survive miraculously. I envisioned the shot going directly through me without causing harm."

Upon entering his first professional game, this invincibility, supernatural ability, and supreme confidence would see him through. "Some veterans would shake with nervous energy before each game," Lem says. "Before one of our games, Alex Karras actually gave up his lunch before telling me, 'If you play this game and don't get some butterflies, you'd better get out.'

"I never experienced that kind of pre-game nervousness, but there were certainly those first initial moments in the game where butterflies would churn inside of me. But apart from those pesky butterflies, I was not afraid. I doubt that anyone who experienced fear in the game could stay in the game."

No fear indeed.

Respect, yes.

Reverence for the opponent? Probably.

But fear? Forget about it. Lem was no cowardly Lion.

Lemuel Barney II was about to be christened into the NFL, experiencing his professional baptism in this holy church of a stadium where the presiding high priest's name was synonymous with success, professionalism and great accomplishments: Packers quarterback Bart Starr.

As the mighty Packers took possession of the ball, Lem made his way to the huddle of old Lions, veterans, and colorful characters. "In the huddle, some of the vets offered me advice," Lem says. "I remember Alex Karras telling me to just play my game.

Easier said than done. "I was in awe of the Packers," Lem says. "They had people like Starr, Paul Hornung, Herb Adderley, and were coached by Mr. Vince Lombardi. They were also the defending Super Bowl champions." The Packers' first play went nowhere, and Starr went back to the huddle. The Packers, especially Starr and Lombardi, had a habit of going right after a rookie to test his mettle. But Lem was prepared.

As Starr broke from the huddle and lined up over center, he surveyed the defense. Like a lion eyeing his prey before a kill, Starr focused his attention immediately on the young Lion cornerback. Hunting for first-down yardage, Starr dropped back and looked in the direction of receiver Carroll Dale.

Lem remembers the scene. "Now it's second and seven, wide side of the field," he says. "Starr did a three-step drop and planned a quick out throw to Dale. I read the play and Starr saw me closing on Dale. As Starr released the ball, it was his intent to throw the pass low and away so it wouldn't be intercepted. His pass was on the mark, low and away from Dale, but I managed to get inside Dale and dive about five yards, intercepting the pass. Springing to my feet, I ran the ball into the Packer end zone for a 24-yard touchdown." As Lem scored that touchdown, he spiked the ball into the ground, looked up and exclaimed, "Lord, is this going to be easy."

"I was mobbed by my teammates after that play," Lem remembers. "The scene was pure pandemonium. To score on a play like that, in your first game, on the first throw in your direction, seemed more like a Hollywood script." Cecil B. DeMille could not have written it any better for Lem.

Longtime Detroit sportswriter Jerry Green remembers it well. "The Packers had won the very first Super Bowl ever and were the champions," he says. "Starr looked to his right and saw this rookie, and I think he threw the pass to Carroll Dale. Lem stepped in front of Dale, did a somersault, and ran twenty-four yards for a touchdown on the very first play he ever covered."

Green looked at his colleagues in the press box and told them that Barney kid would never be able to match his first play in the pros. "But Lem Barney proved me and a lot of other people wrong," he says. "He intercepted ten passes his rookie season and he became an All-Pro and rookie of the year."

Lem was ecstatic then and still is today whenever he remembers it. "First play and I score a touchdown against the Green Bay Packers by picking off a pass by the great Bart Starr," he says. "I felt weightless. I remember that day like it was yesterday ... but it was nearly thirty-nine years ago. Playing professional football was never easy, but it was always fun."

After the game, Lem received congratulations from his teammates and opponents alike. One special encounter was with Packers defensive back Herb Adderley. "The game ended in a 17-17 tie," Lem says. "I remember running over to the Green Bay bench and introducing myself to Herb. I told him that I wore his number 26 at Jackson State because I was a huge fan of his. I shook his hand and told him I'd like to become half as good a player as he was. He grabbed my hand and said, 'Don't worry, just keep playing like you're playing now, and you'll become as good a player as me, or even better.' I was thrilled."

Hearing something like that from one of his heroes had Lem flying high. How far he would travel and what kind of landing he would have seemed to be the only questions that left fans, writers, and players unsure. But one thing was evident with his play; the rookie from the small southern college had brought excitement back to the gridiron and captured the interest and imagination of Lions fans everywhere. With his stellar debut, there was once again hope in Motown for a franchise that would soon see better days. Lem was sending a message to the lion-hearted everywhere. "Lord, is this going to be fun."

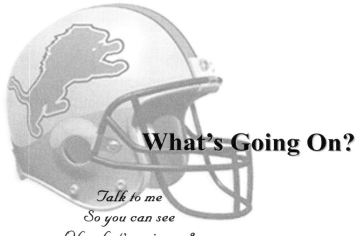

What's Going On?

Talk to me
So you can see
Oh, what's going on?
Yeah, what's going on?
Ah, what's going on?

—*Marvin Gaye, 1971*

*I*N HIS SECOND YEAR AS A LION, LEM had become so comfortable in Detroit that he decided to introduce himself to Marvin Gaye, his musical hero. But he had to find Marvin first. He had been told by teammates that many of them, as well as other notable Detroit personalities, could be found playing golf at Palmer Park. Lem was not yet a golfer himself, but he headed to the course just the same. Cornering the clubhouse boy, Lem introduced himself and asked if Gaye ever played at the course. "I was told that Marvin had just finished up his round and was on his way home," Lem says.

Lem, a lifelong lover of music, then asked the clubhouse boy where Gaye lived. After getting directions, Lem promptly took to the streets. "I usually didn't do things like that," he says. "That was a little forward for me, especially since I was just a young kid." But Lem thought he'd take a chance. "I really respected Marvin and his music," he says. "Besides, I was feeling a little cocky and good about myself, being drafted by the Lions and all."

Lem remembers their first encounter like it was yesterday. "I was nervous," he says. After navigating the mostly unfamiliar streets leading to Gaye's home, Lem walked up to his front door and knocked. "To my great surprise, the door opened and there stood the man I had so often seen on TV and record album covers—the man who made all of the great music I'd come to love. Marvin Gaye in person."

Lem could barely speak.

"Hello, he said. "I'm Lem Barney with the Detroit Lions and I'm a big fan of yours. I just wanted to come by to see if I could meet you."

Gaye flashed his million-seller smile. "Hi, Lem," he said. "I've heard about you. What's goin' on?"

And with that, Lem was invited inside.

"We forged a relationship right there and ended up being close friends over the years," Lem says. "We enjoyed golfing, praying, and singing, and shared many laughs and a few tears together. For the next several years, Marvin, Mel Farr, and I spent a lot of time together and became like brothers."

One night in 1971, says Lem, "the three of us were together and ended up making a little history of our own." Recording history, that is. "During the evening, Marvin was talking about recording a new single... We had been golfing together and Marvin asked someone, 'What's going on?' The three of us agreed right there that that would be a great name for a song."

Farr remembers the night with equal fondness. "Initially, Marvin was planning on giving that song to the Fantastics, another local group," he says. "But Lem and I urged him not to. We suggested instead that Marvin do it himself." After some thought, Gaye agreed, but with one condition. He wanted Mel and Lem to provide background vocals. They quickly agreed.

After a few beers to loosen up at Marvin's house the newly formed trio headed over to the studio, where Lem and Mel settled in and got down to their new business—show business. There, they proceeded with the great Marvin Gaye to lay down the tracks on a tune that would become the classic Motown hit "What's Going On?"

"We were just having fun at that point," Lem says. "We had no idea of the impact that song and album would ultimately have on so many people for so many years." The song became a Motown standard that eventually sold a lot of records. But for Lem, Mel, and many others, it meant far more than that.

"'What's Going On' was a socially conscious artistic effort emanating from the body and soul of a visionary who cried out to the masses to take notice of each other by reaching out across color lines to treat each other with a little more human kindness," Lem says. "It was a great song. We were just proud to be on it. We had just been singing and carrying on with our great friend Marvin and ended up being part of a gold record. That whole experience was like scoring a touchdown with two good friends at your side."

Lem's voice trailed off and after a short pause, he was back in song, to the familiar refrain of bygone days:

Mother, mother
There's too many of you crying
Brother, brother, brother
There's far too many of you dying
You know we've got to find a way
To bring some lovin' here today

Father, father
We don't need to escalate
You see, war is not the answer
For only love can conquer hate
You know we've got to find a way
To bring some lovin' here today

Picket lines and picket signs
Don't punish me with brutality
Talk to me, so you can see
Oh, what's goin' on?
What's goin' on?
Yeah, what's goin' on?
Ah, what's goin' on?

That's Our Boy

"Your children need your presence more than your presents."
—Jesse Jackson

THEY HAD NEVER SEEN HIM PLAY AS A professional athlete. They heard the good things that their boy was doing in the north. For sure, they read the press clippings that Lem sent them. But today was different. Today they could see with their own eyes and feel with their own hearts what good deeds their boy was doing in the name of the Detroit Lions.

Mom and Dad Barney made their way into the big, white, aging stadium at the corner of Michigan and Trumbull. Much like the city in which it was located, Tiger Stadium had seen better days. It certainly could have used a fresh coat of paint and some tender loving care. That much was evident to Mr. and Mrs. Barney as they took a first look at the place where their only son earned his daily bread. The Barney family settled into their seats in the cavernous home of the Detroit Lions and the Detroit Tigers.

"Mom and Dad were very excited about getting a chance to see me play in person," Lem says. "They had never seen me play in a live professional game. I was a little excited, too. You know it's your Mom and Dad. If you can't get excited about that, what can you get excited about?"

† Lem Barney †

The scene was set. 1967. The last game of Lem's rookie season, and the archrival Minnesota Vikings were in town. For years, the Vikings had manhandled the Lions. Over one six-and-half year period, they beat the Lions 13 straight times.

On this cold winter day, the prospects of watching their son and his team succeed did not look promising to the Barneys. But Lem was going to try to make his parents' trip to the Motor City a memorable one. "Every child wants to do well in front of his parents," Lem says. "And of course, I wanted to do something special to make them proud. My spirit was high for this game. It was even more special because it was a divisional game with the Vikings."

As the fourth quarter approached, the Lions and Vikings found themselves embroiled in a typically tight black-and-blue division struggle. It was a game where both teams played classic hard, tough Central Division football. But it was also the type of game that the Vikings always managed to win.

This day would be different, though, because the rookie from Gulfport was raring to go. On this very special day, he committed football thievery worthy of an old pro safecracker, as his mom, dad, and over 50,000 other crazed and amazed Lion fans watched.

First, Lem picked off an errant Joe Kapp pass and scampered 71 yards for a touchdown. Then he picked off a second pass and ran it back to the Vikings' three-yard line. Then, as if that wasn't enough, Lem picked off a third Kapp pass for good measure, sealing a rare 14-3 victory over the Vikings. What was perhaps most amazing was that he did it all in just one quarter.

One of the Detroit papers ran this headline the next day:

LEM BARNEY 14
VIKINGS 3

Three interceptions in one game would be enough for most players. Still, the three interceptions didn't satisfy Lem. "I really should have had six interceptions in that game, but I dropped three," he insists.

While he might have regretted dropping three potential interceptions, he obviously had no regrets about his parents making the long trip up north to watch him play football in the pros. "Mom and Dad had a good ol' time," he says. "It was a special day for all of us. It was a blessing that they were there to witness it." As most Lions fans made their way out of Tiger Stadium and to their cars, as that 1967 season closed out, two fans from Mississippi lingered a little longer and stared out at the field. Soon the man wearing No. 20 came over to greet them. Mom and Pop Barney didn't need to say a word. They were beaming with pride.

Lem has taken some kidding from the Vikings about that day, including Kapp. "Joe has told me over the years, 'Hey, man, I put you in the Hall of Fame single-handedly,'" Lem says. And while his coaches, teammates, parents, and Kapp may have helped him get there, the young man with the big talent and bigger desire got there on his own.

FOOTPRINTS III

His stance was solid, his muscles tight. As the young man glided down the field, he could see it all out there in front of him. His vision was a perfect 20-20. His eyes were bright, his stride had purpose. His gait not a cocky one, but one that exuded attitude—a swagger associated with champions.

His chosen field was athletics—namely, football. After many years of training, he was about to make it to the big time as a professional football player. As he strode along the grass, he thought about that a moment. And as he did, he had a special consultation with the greatest of all his coaches—his Heavenly Father.

As he fell to his his knees, Lem Barney asked his Maker for guidance.

"Lord, I ask for your blessing and your guidance as I pursue these things on both the football field and the field of life. In Your name, thy will be done if it is Your will."

Then he rose to his feet and sprinted down the field. Once. Twice. Three times. Repeating this again and again on a hot, sun-soaked afternoon, young Lem hardly broke a sweat. The drill was the same. Always the same. But he accepted the routine good-naturedly. Practice and discipline. They were the building blocks of his life on and off the football field.

The young man focused on his target and then ran hard after it. Nothing could stop him now. His greatness lay within his grasp. And as he ran hard toward the goal line, he looked to the heavens to give thanks for his God-given talents and for the direction he received in his life.

"Thank you, Lord, for pointing me in the right direction and for the ability to head there in a swift manner." The sun on the practice field was still high in the sky, as the rookie had completed his afternoon workout. He would go home and rest, as he had to return after sunset for his evening practice. There was still much work to be done.

The sun shone bright, as young Lem sauntered off the field and mopped the sweat off his brow. There wasn't a cloud in the sky. It was completely blue. The aroma of fresh cut grass filled the air.

As the young man left the field, he paused to look back at the goal line. A soft, satisfying smile came across his lips. He knew he was on his way.

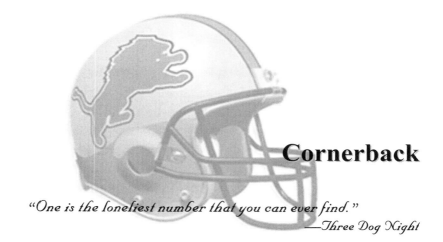

Cornerback

"One is the loneliest number that you can ever find."
—Three Dog Night

A CORNERBACK IS LIKE A PALACE GUARD—the last line of defense, a man whose job it is to stop some of the most talented players in the world from doing their job. It's the loneliest position on a football field—a virtual no man's land, where the task is to make sure that no man beats you for a big play that could cost your team the game. To call the cornerback position just another pressure-packed job is to call Shakespeare just another playwright.

Cornerback is where you're most apt to go from a goat to a star and back again on successive plays. When you play there, you'd better leave your indecisiveness at home. A cornerback is asked to throw blanket coverage over the biggest, fastest, swiftest athletes in the world, all of whom have a distinct advantage over the lonely defensive back.

The receiver knows all along where the ball is going. The cornerback does not. His only hope is that he'll get there in time to break up the play.

Cornerbacks are like cops trying to bust up crimes committed by two criminals—a quarterback and a receiver, whose job is to steal six points. Every time a ball enters the cornerback's territory, it's either sink or swim.

Like an overworked beat cop, the cornerback relies on his speed, his wits, and sometimes, a little help from above to make the big play and prevent disaster. This is where Lem excelled. His job was to stymie the NFL's best receivers—all-stars like Washington's Bobby Mitchell, Green Bay's Carroll Dale, and Dallas' Lance Alworth. It was a role Lem filled like no one before him. He intercepted fifty-six passes during his eleven seasons with the Lions, second only to Dick LeBeau in club history. Ten of those pickoffs came as a rookie in 1967 when Lem led the league, and before teams learned it was foolhardy to throw on him. Still, five times during his career, Lem finished the season as Detroit's top pass thief.

"During his era, he was one of the best at his position," Mitchell says. "Lem came in with a group that could really run in the secondary. You had not seen very many defensive backs with the speed he had. With the ability to cover from sideline to sideline, he ushered in an era of speed that we had not previously seen."

In the NFL's long history, there were few players who were as good as Lem, the cornerback with the quick feet and a penchant for the big play. There were even fewer who could get one over on him.

"The only way to beat him was to be perfect," Dale says.

To beat Lem, receivers would have to run precise routes and make circus catches to commit the perfect crime against a gambling, bump-and-run ball-hawk. Problem was, for most receivers, Lem was seldom asleep on the job.

"Every time he lined up, he challenged himself," says Hall of Fame Packers defensive end Willie Davis. "To Lem, the ball was just as much his as the receiver's. He was fundamentally sound and reminded me a lot of Herb Adderley."

Alworth remembers what it was like to go up against Lem. "He was a great athlete and one of the very best to ever play the position," he says.

The occupation of stopping these ball-catching studs was something the studious Barney took home with him. "The only way to do the job is to do the work, and a big part of the work is on the practice field," he says. Lem followed legendary Lion Dick "Night Train" Lane at his position. "Night Train was a big man with big shoes to fill," Lem says. "He was one of my heroes, one of my mentors who I learned the game from, learned the position from, and I owe him a lot for showing me how to play the game."

Lem also owes his gratitude to Lions coach Joe Schmidt and assistant coach Jimmy David. Both men had a profound influence on his stellar career. "Lem had the same thing Night Train had," David says. "If a man got a step on him, he had the quickness to get over to cover before the ball got there."

Lem believes the support he got from his coaches made the transition to the pro game much smoother for him. "From the beginning, I had the opportunity to demonstrate my skills, talents, and attributes," he says. "I can remember Coach Schmidt saying, 'I'm not going to ask you to do anything out of your realm. I'm asking you to do things within your means. If you give me all you have on every play, we're going to have fun and we're going to win.'"

Like all great players, Lem was a student of the game, and he examined all his opponents intently. "We derived a game plan for every situation," he says. "First and ten, second and short, third and long..." Lem and his teammates learned what plays had worked for their opponents and studied their tendencies. "If they did it over the last five games," he says, "they were going to do it in the sixth ballgame as well. When I recognized their routes, it gave me a jump on the effort to move in and break up the play. It could even put me in a good position to intercept the ball."

Lem will never forget the thrill of the kill—picking off a pass. "It's quite exhilarating when you make that decision because the outcome of a game is on the line, and it becomes a contest just between you and the receiver," he says. "The winner is a hero and the loser is guilty of poor judgment."

Veteran Detroit News football writer Mike O'Hara says that Lem brought unique talents to the position, revolutionizing the backpedal technique with his quick feet and long strides. "Watching Lem work was like watching a high-speed film," O'Hara says. "His feet were just a blur. He was definitely one of the top five NFL players at that position. I'll remember him as 'The Supernatural' who reacted instantly when he heard a little voice inside, directing him to make his move. When he heard that little voice, he reacted."

To Lem, the entire process was instinctive. "Making that move towards an interception represents a fine line between being able to get into position, versus running the risk of being a little late—and watching your opponent streak into the end zone and maybe costing your team a victory. The difference is so minute."

That didn't happen to Lem often. But it did happen.

"When you go for the interception and fail, it feels like everyone in the stadium is throwing garbage on you," he says. "When you decide to gamble and the gamble doesn't pay off, you become your own worst critic.

"Freddie Biletnikoff beat me twice on Thanksgiving Day, when he made two great post-corner moves, and I went in. He broke just right and the passes were thrown perfectly. He won, and I was left feeling like a rookie."

"I remember that day," says former Detroit News columnist Jerry Green. "Lem was great, but on that day, he was not unbeatable. Lem was, after all, just human and Biletnikoff was one darn good football player. That's why they're now both in the Hall of Fame."

Most days, Lem was the one who got the best of his opponents, frequently turning his ball-hawking skills into six points for Detroit. Seven times during his career, he returned an interception for a touchdown. Three of those came during his rookie season, and two more in 1970, as Lem helped the Lions reach the playoffs for their first appearance since 1957.

"He was always one of the players you needed to be aware of at all times," says Miami Dolphins Hall of Fame quarterback Bob Griese. "Playing with a talented guy like [receiver] Paul Warfield, I would often just throw the ball up and let him beat the corner. But when you went up against Lem, you'd better check—and double-check, just to be safe. Lem was a risk-taker and would often go for the interception."

Hall of Fame Cleveland Browns tight end Ozzie Newsome believes Lem would still be an all-star at his position in today's NFL. "When you look at the corners that are playing the game today, you quickly realize that Lem had the same type of athleticism that those guys do," Newsome says. "He had outstanding quickness, the ability to change direction, great ability to close, and the knack for making the big play at the right time."

Lem credits his coach and friend Jimmy David for helping him develop into a nearly unbeatable corner. "Jimmy played the same position, and the little things he would teach me made all the difference," Lem says. "He worked you hard, and I respected that." Both men agree that playing the game well takes hard work, and David's practices set the stage for real competition. In his playing days, David was called "The Hatchet Man." He put everything he had into defeating you when you were in his corner.

Dolphins Hall of Fame coach Don Shula, a former Lions assistant, saw something special every time he watched Lem work the corner. "Lem had all the qualities," Shula says. "He was very bright, athletic, competitive, and very physical—all the things you look for in a…defensive back, packaged into one body."

On the corner, Lem was more about crime than punishment. "I was a finesse player," he says. "Players like Ronnie Lott or Jack Tatum played the position differently. They just liked to rip up ball carriers. My strategy was to tie up a runner's legs and bring him down in less than five yards. It would then be second down and five, and I had not suffered a dislocated shoulder or other injury in the process."

A sensational coverage guy, Lem employed a different technique tackling running backs. "I always tried to be part of a gang tackle on great runners," he says. "The league had some very strong runners during those years, but we had a pretty good defense, particularly against the run. But as good as we were, Walter Payton still managed to gain 263 yards on us at Thanksgiving. And O.J. Simpson broke his own [single-game rushing] record against us. But these were the exceptions."

Two of the greatest corners to play the game, fellow Hall of Famers Lott and Mel Blount, idolized Lem. "He was my hero, and I say that with all sincerity," Blount says. "I've never seen an athlete with feet as quick as his. He had the smoothest backpedal and the fastest feet. I think pound-for-pound, he's one of the best defensive backs that ever played the game."

Lott agrees. "When Lem played defense, he was also playing offense. Being able to catch the ball and being able to score with it says a lot about how he thought about the game. There aren't many defensive ballplayers that have the Barney mindset, believing they can score on any given play."

Although he played a different style of football, Lem could still appreciate the play of his fellow defensive backs, including Oakland's Jack Tatum. "He played tough and he hit hard," Lem says. "I don't believe that he ever intended to do any serious bodily harm to anyone or ever intended to cause the damage to Darryl Stingley that he did." (Patriots wide receiver Stingley was left paralyzed after a jarring hit from Tatum in a 1978 preseason game). Tatum was just trying to do his job. Sadly, Stingley had been playing without a neck support that day."

Hall of Fame Dallas Cowboys defensive back Mel Renfro remembers his friend's ability to make the big plays. "Lem had great technique and style and had the athletic ability to make important individual plays even when his team was not winning," Renfro says. "He always came to the game ready to play. His attitude, tenacity, and commitment were admired by other teams and players alike."

For opposing quarterbacks, Lem's presence on the other side of the ball was a nightmare. Former New York Giants quarterback Y.A. Tittle remembers dealing with Lem. "He was one of the better defensive backs in the NFL," Tittle says. "There's no doubt about that. The corner position is the toughest to play. If you make a mistake, it's going to result in a touchdown. You cannot win games without two good corners. And with Lem, the Lions had one of the best."

Former Minnesota Vikings safety Paul Krause holds the NFL record for most career interceptions (eighty-one). He, too, can't forget what it was like to play against Lem. "I know that our receivers didn't want to play into his corner," he says. "Lem was as good as it gets. He had quick feet, great reaction to the ball, and wasn't afraid to make a tackle."

Playing the corner opposite Lem was Dick LeBeau. He holds the Lions' franchise interception record with sixty-two. "Dick was an edgy ballplayer," Lem says. "He was intuitive about the game and very much willing to help me improve. He was also a great believer in studying the opposition and knowing what the receivers were going to do."

Roger Staubach remembers what a tough defense the Lions had. "Back then, everybody knew Lem was good," he says. "You just did not mess around with him." With Lem in the game, the Lions could play a lot of man-to-man defense—especially on blitzes—which gave the team a great deal of flexibility. "Some players could not play man-to-man on a blitz," Staubach says, "but Lem could do it all. He was a good tackler, but more importantly, he was a good team leader. He was just the kind of guy you would want on your football team."

Joe Hoskins, Lem's teammate at Jackson State, knows that better than most. "He was the very best of all time while he was here," he says. "I'm always on the lookout for Lem's qualities in my students."

Former Lion Charlie Sanders, one of the best tight ends in NFL history, had the tough task of facing Lem every day in practice. "I think he was the prototype for his position," Sanders says. "He had great speed and toughness and was a great athlete. The greatest play I ever saw him make was against the all-star receiver from the New York Jets, Don Maynard, who was one of the best of the best. Lem actually let the receiver catch the ball and then took it out of his hands. That play says it all."

Former defensive back Jim Thrower, who played with and against Lem, likens him to a modern-day superstar. "He was like Deion Sanders," Thrower says. "He just dared quarterbacks to throw it his way."

Baltimore Colts Hall of Fame running back/flanker Lenny Moore remembers his last—and Lem's first—year in the league. And what he saw made a lasting impression. "I was aware that he was going to become one of the best defensive backs in the game," Moore says. "You could see that from his overall ability to cover opposing players. When I was trying to run a couple of pass patterns on him, he covered me like glue."

His years in the NFL, the routes, the receivers, the broken plays, and the interceptions have given Lem the opportunity to meet and to know many of his opponents. "I knew Night Train Lane and the late, great Emlen Tunnell from the New York Giants. Emlen had scouted me at Jackson State and wanted me to become a Giant."

Tunnell got his wish, all right. Lem, in fact, turned out to be a giant Detroit Lion.

Dizzying Madness: The Punt Returner

"Fine art is that which the hand, the head, and the heart
of a man go together."

—John Ruskin

WHAT WAS IT LIKE WATCHING LEM Barney return a punt? It was dizzying madness.

Watching Lem Barney return a punt was like being on a roller coaster, a tilt-a-whirl, and a slip-and-slide all at the same time. It was like trying to catch a snake with two spoons, or a moth with chopsticks.

While his legs churned beneath him, Lem's body moved in different directions at the same time, while still planted on the ground. The blur of motion was more cartoon character than football player. Lem could have been the model for Warner Brothers' Roadrunner. Like the Roadrunner, Lem drove NFL predators crazy, much the way the Roadrunner affected poor Wile E. Coyote. So often, he left opposing players grasping at air.

Whenever Number 20 went back to return a punt, there was always a good chance he'd make Howard Cosell's Monday Night Football halftime highlights. "He scared his opponents to death," says former Minnesota Viking Paul Krause. "You never wanted him to … even get his hands on the ball."

On a September 27, 1970, the Cincinnati Bengals made that mistake, and it resulted in one of the most spectacular punt returns in NFL history. The Lions were comfortably ahead 24-0 in the second quarter, when Bengals punter Dave Lewis lofted the ball downfield. It hit the Tiger Stadium turf at the Lions' 39-yard-line, and four Bengals surrounded the ball, ready to down the pigskin when it completed its roll. Just then, quick as a flash, Lem darted between the stunned Bengals defenders and scooped up the ball in one motion. Sixty-one yards later, he was standing in the Cincinnati end zone.

"We had set up the short-side return, and for an instant, everybody on the Cincinnati team just stood there waiting for the whistle to blow," Lem says. "I glanced up the field and saw lots of blocking. So I grabbed the ball, jockeyed myself free from the traffic, and started to run. I got a couple of blocks and just ran to daylight."

That was the way Lem could electrify a crowd, even on a seemingly mundane play. Long before Deion Sanders, Lem was putting on a prime time show every time he touched the ball. When Lem went back to field a punt, people moved to the edge of their seats.

"When Lem had the ball," former DETROIT NEWS writer Joe Falls once said, "he was like the national anthem. He made people stand up." Lem performed on the edge, with catlike quickness and moves that would leave James Brown green with envy.

And while the term *fair catch* could not usually be used in the same breath as Lem's name, he actually holds the record of seven fair catches in one game. But that's not the way most people remember him. When Lem's opponents sent their punt coverage team on the field, they did so with trepidation. Their entire focus was on Number 20, who stood waiting with one thing on his mind: doing something spectacular.

Sportswriter Jerry Green recalls a game where Lem fielded a punt at his one-yard line. "He picked it up and used his hand to whip himself around the goal post and start the other way," Green says. "It was remarkable."

Heaven, to Lem, was a football flying through the sky and falling into his arms, as the opposing team bore down on him. A move to the left, then to the right, and a fake as he made the first tackler miss. Just like Barry Sanders, the original Number 20 almost always made the first man miss. The others missed early and often. Lem would zig and zag, juke and jive, exhausting his pursuers, just as he exhausted the vocabulary of those in the press box.

In 1970, Lem averaged an astonishing 21.2 yards per punt return, making it almost reasonable for the opposition to gamble on fourth down rather than kick to him. "Lem was an exceptional player," says Hall of Fame linebacker Ted Hendricks. "I've had the opportunity of watching him intercept passes and run back punts. His talents were amazing. He could run and do it all."

Lem could unite and excite any crowd. He could bring white-collar automotive executives from suburbia and blue-collar assembly workers from Downriver out of their seats. Their voices still echo today at old Tiger Stadium. As they watched him run back a punt in his Honolulu blue and white jersey, they all stood in unison.

Lem often brought Lions fans out of their seats, as they marveled at his antics. With jaw-dropping looks of disbelief, fans and writers struggled to find the words to describe him. Like a prima ballerina, a renowned tenor, or a master painter, Lem was an athlete with an artistically flamboyant spirit, who displayed his masterpieces on the field.

Calling All Pros

"When I played pro football, I never set out to hurt anybody deliberately. Unless it was, you know, important —like a league game or something."

—Dick Butkus

L EM BARNEY PLAYED WITH SOME OF THE best players ever to play the game. And he joined a very elite club—the Pro Football Hall of Fame, a fraternity to which only a select few are chosen. And while Lem himself was great, he also recognized greatness.

For seven out of his eleven years in the league, Lem was an All-Pro. It wasn't a Pro Bowl unless the great Number 20 from Detroit made the journey to play in the game. And each time he was chosen, Lem went excitedly, willingly, to show off his skills.

"I loved playing in the Pro Bowl with all the best of the NFL," he says. "I missed out when they permanently moved the Pro Bowl to Hawaii. But I really didn't care where the game was being played. I was just honored and happy to be playing in it."

Fellow Hall of Fame defensive back Mel Renfro recalls Lem's All-Pro ability. "In those days, All Pros were selected by fellow players, peers, and coaches—with little input from the media," he says. "Lem's regular selection to this elite group clearly indicated what his fellow NFL players thought of his skills. Many thought he was clearly head and shoulders above the rest."

Lem was one of the best in the Class of '67. But he was not alone. Five other Hall of Famers came out of the same draft, including Dolphins great Bob Griese. "Griese was a remarkable quarterback," Lem says, "even though he didn't get much early recognition. He was both a great quarterback and coach on the field. He had a real sense and a great feel for the game."

And then there was division rival Alan Page, a fierce Vikings defensive lineman, who graduated from Notre Dame. "He created nightmares for Lions quarterbacks," Lem says. "I managed to just edge him out for the 1967 Defensive Rookie of the Year Award, but he'll be judged as one of the best players ever at his position."

Today Page serves on the Minnesota state Supreme Court.

Another "classmate" of Lem's was longtime Oakland Raiders guard Gene Upshaw, who broke into the league in 1967. Lem sees Upshaw as a man of honor and veracity. And he's not alone. Today, Upshaw serves as the leader of the NFL Players Association.

And then there was Willie Lanier. "Willie was the first African-American to play the middle linebacker position," Lem says. "He was a great man and a great ballplayer." A fellow Southwestern Athletic Conference graduate and Hall of Famer from Morgan State, Lanier brought light to his friend Lem's path to the NFL and later in life. Today, Lanier remains proud of Lem's accomplishments and others like him—products of traditional black colleges who were later inducted into the Hall of Fame.

"Like Lem and many others from the same background, we attained recognition because the starting point of our mutual expectations was probably zero." Coming from those small black schools, players like Lanier and Lem had a sense of urgency—an understanding that they had to perform right away. "Lem is a classic example," Lanier says. "He's classy, skillful, savvy, and a charismatic kind of person who has taken his immense athletic gifts and blended them with his ministerial work. That's an awesome accomplishment."

Lem is still quite fond of former Oilers and Redskins safety Kenny Houston, who is yet another Hall of Famer and member of the

Class of '67. "You want to play with four guys like Kenny every week," Lem says. "He was as tough as anyone in the league. He studied the game and was as strong a strong safety as you'll see."

Houston, of course, was a fan of Lem's, too. "At the time, Lem had the fastest backpedal in professional football," Houston says. "He was flashy, yet very humble … he was a guy who stood out, even in a room full of All-Pros. As a matter of fact, he stands out as a Hall of Famer in a room full of Hall of Famers."

Houston saw how gifted Lem was and always tried to learn something from him at the Pro Bowl every year. "I can still see him today backpedaling. Lem was fluid, and he could get your attention. Professionals stopped and watched as he did his job, and that's the ultimate respect."

Lem faced some legendary competitors throughout his storied career. As a rule, he respected them all—but never feared them. "Gale Sayers was so special," he says. "He was a very elusive runner who some people forget was one of the great kick and punt return artists of all time."

And then there was perhaps the greatest ever—the enigmatic Jim Brown. "Jimmy Brown took the game from an artistic level to a scientific level," Lem says. "He was doing things that had never been done before. He had speed, quickness … and he was shifty—simply a great football player." And though Lem never played against Brown, he still referred to Lem as "the great warrior."

Lem remembers Brown paying him what he at first thought was a tribute. "I was playing golf with him one day when he said that it would've been nice if he had played against me. He said that he had watched that 'stuff I had in my shoes.' I thought he was paying me a compliment and I agreed that such a matchup would have been great. But with that famous Brown deadpan, he said, "'No, I mean playing against your butt, man.'"

Lem's warrior-like qualities are echoed by fellow All-Pro teammate Charlie Sanders. "On the field, he was always on top of the game," Sanders says. "The league adopted a new rule stating that, if on a punt, the ball had been touched, you could advance it. Well, the next week, Lem used the new rule to advance the ball for a touchdown. To truly appreciate Lem Barney, all you have to ask is, 'What can't he do?' He can even sing like an All-Pro."

So what does Lem look for when he's looking for something great or supernatural in an athlete? "The special quality of an athlete is displayed in the fundamentals and how they're executed," he says. "It's the fundamentals that are going to help you win or lose the game. Utilizing fundamentals, your principles, and the mechanics of the game is the approach that makes a good ballplayer a great ballplayer. You can recognize the quality of a defensive back by his backpedaling. And the same fundamentals apply for players of any position. Are they running good, crisp routes—not rounding them off, but squaring them off and running them to the spot?"

Based on his knowledge of football, the players of the game, and the nature of the competition, Lem has often thought of his NFL dream team. "There are many great players who've played this game," he says. "It's difficult to name just a few, but I'll try. At quarterback, I would pick Fran Tarkenton. Tarkenton was not the biggest guy, but he was tough to play against. In the backfield would be O.J. Simpson, Walter Payton, Eric Dickerson, Chuck Foreman, Larry Csonka, and of course, Barry Sanders. At wide receiver, I would pick Paul Warfield and Charlie Taylor. At tight end, I would pick Charlie Sanders—our Detroit guy. Charlie belongs in the Hall of Fame, and I hope that he gets there soon. All of these guys were the best because of speed, quickness, and the execution of fundamentals."

On the offensive, line Lem picks fellow Jackson State alumni Jackie Slater, who spent his entire career with the Rams, alongside Miami's Larry Little, Oakland's Gene Upshaw, and Cincinnati's Rufus Mayes and Anthony Muñoz. Lem won't soon forget the imposing presence of Mayes. "He was 6-foot-9, about 275 or 280, and was from Ohio State," Lem says. "I caught a knee from him in the right side of my head one time and was knocked out for about 20 minutes."

Defense, which was Lem's forte, brought these memories. "At linebacker, we played against four greats in the Central Division; Ray Nitschke, Dick Butkus, Ray Seaman, and Mike Lucci. I would take either Butkus or Nitschke in the middle linebacker position. Each would give every ounce in his body to make a play. And Dave Wilcox was a great ballplayer and great man on the outside."

On the defensive line, Lem states without hesitation the one name at the top of his list: "You can give me a Deacon Jones any day," he says. "Deacon was a never-say-die guy. He had tremendous pursuit and an ability to run down running backs and quarterbacks. And because the league did not start keeping stats on sacks until about the middle part of Deacon's career, a lot of them went unrecorded. I think that if sacks had been recorded back then, the league record would have been his forever."

Jones, a great friend and fellow Hall of Famer, hasn't forgotten old No. 20. "Lem and I go back to his rookie year," he says. "He is an open person and has that team personality. He caught my eye while reviewing his films during his first year. He was such a fantastic athlete, not only a great personality, but could he ever cover."

Jones, a ferocious down lineman, also appreciates what it's like to play the backfield. "Playing the corner in the NFL is like being on an island by yourself," he says. "You need speed, quickness, and knowledge. And when you realize that Lem came out of Jackson State, his accomplishments are even more exceptional." Jones maintains that to achieve the level of success that Lem did—while coming from a small black school where the competition was inferior—is simply remarkable. "I would rank Lem right up in the top three of my all-time greats."

When Lem was in man-to-man coverage, there was no light between him and the receiver. He simply personified "blanket coverage." And Jones saw it time and time again from the opposite sideline. "Anywhere the game took Lem on the field, he had heart—and he could tackle like hell. And when we played in All-Star games, I would get Lem in a corner and tell him, 'We have to get you out of Detroit. You deserve, one time in your life, to play with a great defensive line.' And I sure talked to [Los Angeles Rams coach] George Allen many times about trying to get Lem."

Fallen Teammate

*"Any man's death diminishes me, because I am involved in mankind;
and therefore never send to know for whom the bell tolls;
it tolls for thee."*

—*John Donne*

H E WAS LAID UP IN DETROIT'S HENRY Ford Hospital on West Grand Boulevard, unable to play and unable to do much of anything but listen to the radio. His teammates were about to take the field October 24, 1971, to play the Chicago Bears just down the street at Tiger Stadium. The week before, Lem had suffered a torn groin muscle in a tough game against the Houston Oilers, and now he was out of commission.

A frustrated Lem listened intently as he tried to imagine the game without him, tried to picture what was going on between his teammates and Dick Butkus's Bears. He tossed and turned but could not get comfortable in his hospital gown. Missing games was not something that sat well with Lem. So as he tuned in on the radio, he was worried. Not so much about the game, but more about his own physical condition.

Listening to announcer Van Patrick describe the scene down at the corner of Michigan and Trumbull, Lem gazed out his hospital window and thought a lot about his life—and about his most recent injury. The look on his face said it all. "It was the most pain I've experienced in my entire life," he says. Still, he sought to focus his attention on the radio and away from his pain.

There at Tiger Stadium, a typical, hard-fought battle between the bitter rivals was being waged. Smashmouth football—where yards were hard to come by and every gain was accompanied by an extra hit. A game where you played with pain and never, ever complained. A game between the Monsters of the Midway and Detroit's gridiron gladiators.

It was exactly the type of game that Lem lived for, that he hated to miss. "Chicago Bears, Detroit Lions, Tiger Stadium, cold weather.

"What else do you have to say?" he says. A restless, powerless Lem urged his teammates on from his hospital bed.

Patrick described the game to Lem, as he did to every football fan in town:

"Lions trail the Bears, 28-23, late here in the fourth quarter, but the Lions still have one more chance to pull this one out. They have the ball and they have plenty of time."

With the Lions running a two-minute drill, wide receiver Chuck Hughes came into the game. Lem listened intently.

"And here's a pass over the middle ... It's incomplete. "That'll bring up fourth down."

"Shoot!" exclaimed Lem, who was now relegated to the role of fan. There wasn't a thing he could do from his hospital bed but cross his fingers and hope for the best.

Patrick continued:

"Let's see," he said. "There's a Lion down on the field. I can't make out the number. I think it's Chuck Hughes ..."

Hughes had collapsed on his way back to the Lions' huddle. Teammate Charlie Sanders remembers it well:

"It was a third-down passing situation," Sanders says. "We were in a two-minute drill situation, and sometimes a player will fake an injury to stop the clock. The pass was intended for me, but it was incomplete. When I went back to the huddle, I saw Chuck lying on the field, and I thought he was faking an injury to try to kill the clock. But then back in the huddle, we saw a commotion that Dick Butkus was creating, trying to wave people onto the field. He was letting people know it was not a fake injury. Dick Butkus got to Chuck first and alerted our bench. Team doctor Richard Thompson came onto the field and tried to resuscitate him, unsuccessfully."

Lem remembers how helpless he felt in his hospital room.

"The announcers were making small talk about what could have happened," he says. "They really had no idea of what was happening physically to Chuck. None of us did as the emergency medical team rushed him to the hospital."

The game ended in silence.

When Hughes collapsed, the time on the clock had almost expired. Back at Henry Ford Hospital, Lem's pain was replaced with silent concern and prayer for his fallen teammate.

"Anytime someone goes down with an injury, I say a prayer," he says.

Following the game, the Lions waited for word about Hughes' condition. Before the team left the stadium, the announcement came. Hughes had suffered a heart attack—he could not be revived.

"It was devastating," Sanders says. "You remember certain habits a guy has. Chuck had this habit of stretching with a shoestring while always sitting in the same place in the meeting room. Now that chair is vacant and everybody was in shock. It's an eye-opener. It's a realization not only about football, but life in general. When you have a guy 28, 29 years old, he's not thinking about death. He's preparing for the future."

At the memorial service for Hughes, held at a Catholic church in downtown Detroit, a few of the Chicago Bears came to pay their respects. Dick Butkus, the often-misunderstood, soft and cuddly Bear was one of them. "Every time I think back on that moment, I'm nearly overcome by the somber mood that had prevailed, reminding me once more of just how precious life truly is," he says.

Longtime DETROIT NEWS sportswriter Jerry Green was on the scene:

"It was a horrific moment," Green says. "[Hughes] went out for a pass, and in a brief moment, he went down. I can still see Dick Butkus standing over him, urging the Lions bench to get the trainer on the field quickly. It was just like it happened yesterday. I can see the doctor pounding at his chest. After Hughes had been carried from the field, the Lions closed the locker room. A group of players, writers, and others stood outside the clubhouse waiting for word…

"And when the word came, everyone's worst fears were realized. Chuck Hughes died playing the game he loved. The paper sent me, and the entire Lions team also went to San Antonio for Chuck's funeral. After the funeral, Coach [Joe] Schmidt thanked Jack Saylor of the Free Press and me for not being too pushy about reporting the story."

The toll was devastating on the tough men who make their living at this brutal game.

"It was like a bad dream that we all hoped we would awake from," Sanders says. "It was a low point for the NFL and the Lions organization. Hughes' death was something unheard of and something you could not forget about. We knew him and his family well, and he was a part of *our* family."

"It could happen to anybody at anytime," Lem says, "but when a young, healthy athlete dies like that, you have to be reminded that playing football is not the most important game in life."

"Any man's death diminishes me…
…I am involved in mankind…
…For whom the bell tolls, it tolls for thee."
—John Donne

Feeding Time: Feeding the Pride

"Lions are among the highest on the food chain, eating whatever they happen to bring down. Lions may go for several days without food, though they prefer not to. An adult lion requires eleven pounds of meat per day. Unlike many other felines, they are able to capture larger prey, because they hunt in groups."

—*Lion Experts*

WHILE IT'S NOT KNOWN WHETHER MIKE Lucci or Alex Karras actually ate eleven pounds of meat on any given Sunday, it is widely known that once the game was over, many of the Detroit Lions could be seen dining together at one of their favorite restaurants in Detroit. Larco's was a family-run, mom-and-pop Italian restaurant where the battle-scarred Lions would gather as a group to lick their wounds, swap stories, and join in an epicurean hunt for the culinary offerings of the Larco Brothers.

Gus Pappas waited tables at Larco's and recalls how, in the late 1960s, the Lions would put their mark on a corner of the restaurant—territory separated from other diners—and partake of civilized Serengetti Spaghetti.

"They would come in as group, and we would put them in a special place in the restaurant," Pappas says. "I was always amazed at just how much pain they were in. Some would come in on crutches, and they would often have to help each other up the stairs. It remains a vivid image in my mind."

The original Larco's was located at Six Mile and Livernois, near the University of Detroit, and was run by three bothers. "It was a unique place with a personality reflective of three bothers—Nick, Pete, and Mike Larco," Pappas says. "Mike was the flamboyant guy at the door, happy to buy you a drink. Downstairs cutting meat was Nick. He was an excellent meat cutter, but wasn't really good with people."

Rounding out the Larco team that would feed a team of Lions, as well as many other loyal Detroit patrons over the years, was Pete.

"Pete Larco was the food expediter up in the kitchen, mainly yelling food orders to the waiters," Pappas says. "'Pappas, pick up your veal! Get your food!' But behind the gruff exterior was a good guy. He was the guy who would take minestrone soup over to the Lions during practice."

Pleased by that Italian gesture of friendship and respect, the Lions made Larco's their meeting place after home games. Pappas recalls how they marked out the Lions' feeding territory. "The Lions would come in as a group, and we would reserve the bottom floor for them," he says. "They would go downstairs and have their meals privately."

They would often bring their wives with them, and half the team would show up for dinner.

"The day Chuck Hughes died, they were all here," Pappas says. "They were all much different that day, somber, reserved, and more reflective."

Over the years, old Number 20 left a lasting impression on Pappas. "Lem Barney kind of typified what was going on in Motown in those days through his football and music with Marvin Gaye," he says. "Lem was more than just a football player. He had a special style. He was very flashy and flamboyant. He seemed to typify an era and really enjoyed himself. Sometimes, you could even find him in the dining room greeting fans."

And, of course, Pappas still marvels at Lem's prowess on the football field. "Lem was not as large as a lot of the other players," he says. "You would look at him and have to ask yourself, 'How could a guy his size take such a pounding and how could he tackle such large guys on the field?'"

The brotherhood of Detroit Lions liked what these three Larco brothers had cooking. And they liked sharing the dining experience together at this little Italian joint tucked away near some of the same streets where bedlam broke out during the riots of 1967. Here inside the walls of Larco's, they could feel safe and free to be themselves and teammates in every way.

"Coach Schmidt worked to instill a family creed with his players," Lem says. "We would meet at Larco's and have a private dinner in the bottom of the restaurant. We would get to know each other, our teammates' families, and after awhile, the team became our second family. We needed that. It was something I would look forward to after each game. Everybody wanted to come downstairs, and it was a well-attended affair—especially when we'd win. Even Marvin Gaye started coming downstairs to lead us in singing songs."

Mel Farr often thinks back to the days in the Lions den at Larco's. "It was like a family," he says. "Joe Schmidt worked to keep the team close together. We would have parties and often spend an evening out as a team. We were a family and we cared about each other."

Back then, nobody made big money, but Lions like Lem and Mel and Charlie Sanders played the game hard because they enjoyed it so. "It was a family atmosphere," Sanders says. "If you did not go to one of the team events, a veteran player was sure to ask why you had missed it. We won together, and we lost together. That was the way to fully appreciate the team experience."

The family environment gave the players a chance to learn about each other away from football, and it was crucial in the civil rights era and a time of great social change in America—and in Detroit.

"Even to this day," Sanders says, "what I miss most is the camaraderie and the teammates. When guys left the game, it was that family feeling that lasted."

Lem can still taste his favorite mostaccioli and Italian sausage prepared exquisitely by the Larco family. Larco's was, after all, a perfect place for a family to gather, to break bread, to tell jokes, and to create memories.

As head of the Lions family, Joe Schmidt remembers the Larco's experience. "I was brought up playing pro football that way," he says. "After games, we did not disappear. It was expected that you would be with your teammates, and we had a good time together. When we lost, we would get together and contemplate how we could win the next one. That was the feeling I wanted to instill in my players."

Schmidt was a born leader and always set a good example. "Teamwork and problem-sharing are important in any endeavor," he says. "But you must also enjoy your work and your teammates. I did, and I hoped my players did also."

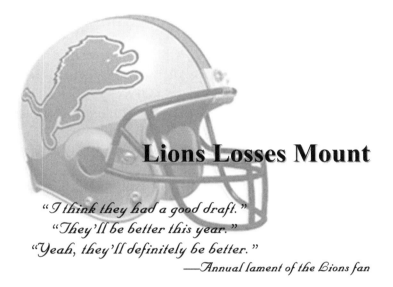

Lions Losses Mount

"I think they had a good draft."
"They'll be better this year."
"Yeah, they'll definitely be better."
—*Annual lament of the Lions fan*

FOR NEARLY 50 YEARS, IF YOU HAPPENED into a Detroit sports bar, you would be able to spot a Lions fan. He was the guy in the corner on Sunday, watching the game on TV, hoping, wishing, and praying that the Lions could complete a pass, block a punt, or make a first down.

In this suffering, Lions fans share a common bond with the men who have played for the team on all of those Sundays over the past half-century. Both fans and players are on the same page when it comes to this sad saga. No soundtrack, no animation, and no happy endings. For them, there was only frustration where the players would change, but the outcome always seemed to remain the same—a streak of endless, disappointing chapters.

As the losses mounted over the years, it became harder to return to the stadium, the TV, or the sports bar. Still they came, both players and fans, united in this brotherhood of Lions loyalty that Chicago Cubs fans can well relate to.

Lions fans across the country come with a hopeful heart and bravely ask the bar owner in Tampa or Texas if they can put the Detroit game on. The bar owner makes a face and pokes fun at such a silly request. If unusually lucky, a Lions fan might find a brother in the bar to share both the pride and pain of his support for the team.

As one loss turns into another, something magical happens. In the heart of the loyal fan, hope still springs eternal. As memories of so many disappointing Sunday afternoon losses fade away, the Lions fan still searches for another lost brother.

"How many yards do you think Barry would have gained had he not retired?"

"Do you think Dempsey's kick should have been blocked?"

"Do you remember when Billy made that catch against Dallas?"

"I wonder how Mike Utley is doing."

"Do you remember how Lem could move and run back a punt?"

The memories flow like a cold Stroh's at the old Lindell AC. That's the nature of the diehard fan's conversation with his brother believers. That's the way such conversations have been for too many years, either for Lions players or fans.

It didn't matter who you were or what your background was. What mattered is that you supported the boys in Honolulu blue and silver. No matter that the result was the same. You were a Lions fan. Whether you played, or just watched, you supported your team. And you did it with hope and pride.

"We had quite a few rookies," Lem says. "Coach Schmidt was trying his best to improve the team and had brought in some good prospects in the hope of rebuilding our lines. While we ended up with a good coaching staff on the sidelines and promising players on the field, we just were not as productive as we wanted to be, or should have been, but we kept at it."

It took four years for Lem to make it to the NFL playoffs. It was a dream come true for him. "We had a great team that year, the best team I ever played on," he says.

Detroit finished 10-4 during that 1970 season, but lost a bitter playoff game to the Dallas Cowboys, 5-0. All the Cowboys could manage was a first-quarter 26-yard field goal from Mike Clark and a fourth-quarter safety, as defensive end George Andrie tackled Lions quarterback Greg Landry in the end zone. The Cowboys limited the Lions to only 178 yards of total offense, while Landry and fellow Detroit QB Bill Munson were just 7-for-20 through the air.

"We did have a great team that year," Schmidt says. "One of the better teams in the league at the time." But his offense was hampered by injuries to running backs Mel Farr and Steve Owens. "But we had a good mixture of experienced and young players," Schmidt says. "It was my first opportunity to be in the playoffs, and we were playing a tough team. I remember that Dallas played their butts off and did not make mistakes. They were out there enjoying themselves."

This was Schmidt's best chance as Lions coach, and as it turned out, the closest that Barney, Farr, and Sanders ever came to playoff success in Detroit. None of them had any way of knowing that at the time, but the knowledge still haunts them years later. "I still replay that game in mind, second-guessing my decisions and playing the what-if game," Schmidt says. "[Earl] McCullough drops a pass that if he catches it, well, it could have…"

The old coach's voice trails off. Perhaps the most talented Lions team since the 1950s, silenced by Tom Landry's Cowboys, 5-0, in what sounds more like a baseball score. Even after more than 35 years, the memory still lingers. "Dallas was a great football team," Schmidt says. "But if we had won the game in Dallas, I would've bet you all the money in the world that we would have been in the Super Bowl game."

Schmidt was never one to make no excuses. And he hasn't changed a bit. "In the end," he says, "I have to take responsibility."

For Lem's football career, only the pain of losing Chuck Hughes eclipses that of the defeat in Dallas. "That was a tough one to lose," Lem says. "We just could not score."

Injuries certainly hurt their chances. "One thing contributing to our loss was the injury to my shoulder that kept me out of the game," Farr says. "It was a wildcard game and for that reason, we did not have a full week off before playing Dallas. I thought we were the best team in the league, but we lost." Farr paused as if the game had just been played, instead of taking place so long ago. "It was just so hard to lose," he says. "We all thought we were playing good enough to win."

The Cowboys advanced to Super Bowl V, losing to the Baltimore Colts, 16-13. But they were in the midst of an eighteen-season run from 1966 to 1983 that saw the club reach the playoffs seventeen times and appear in five Super Bowls, winning twice.

There was no such satisfaction for Lem and the Lions. He would never appear in the playoffs again, nor would the Lions until 1991, fourteen seasons after Lem's career ended. During his eleven seasons in Detroit, Lem enjoyed only four winning campaigns, while breaking even (seven wins, seven loses) in two others. But leave it to Lem to find the silver linings. "In athletics, everybody came together because we wanted to win," he says. "We did not have the best talent, but we wanted so badly to win."

Lem fondly remembers the man who led the Purple People Eaters to all those successes against his Lions. "The Vikings had a way of willing victories to happen," he says. "And it helped that they had a tremendous coach in Bud Grant. The first time I talked with Bud was at the 2000 reunion of the Hall of Fame members. I had a chance to tell him how much I respected and admired the way he generated the respect of his players. His good players ended up being great because of his orders to achieve."

One of those good players became one the best defensive backs to play the game. Viking great Paul Krause remembers his Sundays against Lem's Lions. "They would be ahead of us until the last two or three minutes of the game," Krause says. "Then something would happen and we would be able to come back and beat them. It always seemed that they were going to find a way to lose."

Krause and his Viking teammates always thought Detroit had good personnel, "but something would always get in their way," he says.

Lem painfully agrees. "Minnesota had a winning streak that spanned thirteen games, but those games with us were not blowouts. They would manage to beat us by an extra point, a fumble, a blocked kick, and things like that. I cried a lot in football games against that team. It was upsetting—a demoralizing feeling."

In the last game before the beginning of Minnesota's thirteen-game winning streak, fate was with Detroit. "Near the end of that game, with us leading and the clock running out, Minnesota attempted a desperate Hail Mary pass to John Gilliam in the end zone. I managed to intercept the pass and preserve the win that day." That day, the Vikings were all wearing white shoes and black mustaches, a style Lion players would have liked to adopt. "Until then, Coach Schmidt would not allow it," Lem says. "But with that last interception and win, Coach made an exception and our white shoes and mustaches were soon proudly displayed."

For Lem, his teammates, and Lions fans, some losses hurt more than others. And some losses just didn't seem to make any sense at all. One infamous setback in 1970 qualified on both counts. "It was unforgettable," Lem says.

The game was being played against the New Orleans Saints at Tulane University. The Saints were moving the ball downfield. Following a good pass completion, the Saints were lining up, fourth-and-five on their own 37-yard line in field-goal formation. That would mean their kicker, Tom Dempsey, who was born without a right hand or toes on his right kicking foot and who used a specially designed half-shoe, was about to attempt a 63-yard field goal. At the time, the NFL record for the longest field goal was 56 yards.

"I had played with Dempsey before and watched him hit warmup field goals from the 50-yard line," Lem says. "This day, Dempsey was playing on Astroturf, which seemed to give the ball a little more oomph. Back to the huddle, Mike Lucci and [Alex] Karras thought it was an impossible kick and could not be made. It was my guess that this was going to be a fake kick and a pass. In the huddle, I was told not to go back on pass coverage, but I had a phobia about a fake pass. But I soon realized that he was going to kick because no one broke away from the line of scrimmage."

Even the fleet-footed Lions charging the kicker at full tilt could do nothing to stop the miracle that Dempsey's foot would soon deliver. "As the ball soared up into the air, I retreated toward our goal line," Lem says. "But I only got to our 25-yard line as that ball soared over my head. I thought I could actually hear the sound of the ball spinning as it went over me and cleared the uprights. I often thought later that had I been in a better position on the snap, perhaps I might have had a chance to block it. But then again, if that had happened, Dempsey would not now hold the NFL record of a 63-yard field goal."

New Orleans finished 2-11-1 that season, and Lem remembers the Saints fans and players celebrating the fruits of that victory in fashion similar to a team winning the Super Bowl. "It was the only game I remember where the fans actually came out and tore down the goal posts," he says.

Then the crowd came over and jumped all over Dempsey. During this commotion, somebody stole the shoe right off Dempsey's foot.

"That game was unlike any other I've ever played in," Lem says. "The only other game that was even similar was one we played in Detroit, beating Green Bay (in the last game of the regular season) to make the playoffs in 1970. That was a good year. We managed to beat Green Bay twice by a total of 60 points, 40-0 (in the season opener) and 20-0 in the last game."

In spite of all the losing, it never defeated Lem's winning spirit. "When you go into anything of a competitive nature, you want to be number one," he says. "But everyone can't be the winner. Throughout my years in athletics, from middle school, high school, and the NFL, I was never able to hoist my finger and claim I was number one."

Lem cites his personal accomplishments as his reward, and his determination was evidence of his love of the game. "I have received all-city honors, all-state honors, all-conference, All-American, All-Pro, all-decade team of the 1960s, one of the 100 all-time greatest NFL players, seven Pro Bowls, seven halls of fame, nominated in 2001 as one of Michigan's greatest all-time favorite athletes, but I never won a championship," Lem says.

"But that fact never diminished my effort or will to win. A championship was not in the cards for me during my career, but I did not stick my head in a hole. I held my head high and continued to work as hard as I could to be prepared for whatever was next."

The hard work was noticed and appreciated by other Hall of Famers who played under winning circumstances.

"In football, if you play on a great team like the 49ers or Steelers, there's a good chance your skills will be recognized," says former Pittsburgh Hall of Fame linebacker Jack Ham, a four-time Super Bowl winner.

"When players like Lem Barney make it into the Hall of Fame from teams that did not win championships, that accomplishment is remarkable. It's difficult to always play at a high level when your team only has a 4-8-2 record. That's the reason I have such admiration for a player like Lem Barney."

Ham was surrounded by a cast of top-notch talent in the Steel City. But it wasn't always so for Lem in Detroit. "The quality of play around him did not affect his own," Ham says. "If you were the opponent, you always tried to stay away from Lem Barney. Lem just made too many big plays—just like Mel Blount did here in Pittsburgh."

Blount, a superlative safety in his own right, concurs with Ham. "If we had Lem, we probably would have won seven or eight championships. He could have fit in anywhere."

Jim Taylor and Willie Davis, multiple NFL champions with Vince Lombardi's Green Bay Packers teams of the 1960s, recall the tremendous rivalry between the two Central Division teams. While the Lions didn't always win those contests, they always provided tough opposition.

"The Lions backfield defense was impressive," Davis says. "They sent us home limping many times. I believe that if the Detroit Lions had not been in our division, we would have gone undefeated."

Taylor remembers just how tough the Lions could be on Thanksgiving Day. "The Lions always came onto the field with their collective confidence higher than a kite," Taylor says. "And of course, Lem was always outstanding. In any game, Lem was always prepared, ready, and focused. But on Thanksgiving Day, he became an even better player, if that was possible. It was his overall superb attitude and preparation that made it possible for his induction into the NFL Hall of Fame."

While he could sympathize with Lem, former Cowboys quarterback Roger Staubach could not fully empathize with his plight.

"I was never on a losing team," Staubach says. "I can't relate to that situation. I had the good fortune to be with great players and coaches. I give Lem even more credit for what he accomplished under his circumstances. If Lem had been with the Cowboys, we would have won a few more Super Bowls."

While Lem and his teammates never brought the NFL championship to Detroit, Lem always felt like a champion. In his mind, the difference between a champion and others was clear. "A person who works hard to excel at whatever they may choose to do in life is a champion," he says. "A champion can come from business, public life, or athletics. The mastery of the principles, fundamentals, and mechanics of the game determine a true champion."

Lem and his teammates had a saying. And they repeated it often. "Winners never quit and quitters never win," he says. "When a quitter gives up, it's an admission that they should never have wasted their time, or the time of the competitors in the first place. A person must make up their mind that if they don't go for it, they'll have nothing to show for it."

Lem believes that people who give up can never fulfill their potential. "The Lord does not encourage people to give up," he says. "That surrender demonstrates to everyone that the skills and talents provided by God have not been fully utilized."

Lem points to a man named Job whose job was to never quit. "Job was one of the greatest non-quitters of all time," Lem says. "He possessed what is called intestinal fortitude. Job had what is called stick-to-itiveness. He was never, ever, going to quit."

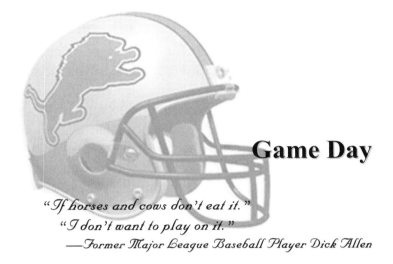

Game Day

"If horses and cows don't eat it."
"I don't want to play on it."
—*Former Major League Baseball Player Dick Allen*

$\mathscr{B}$ACK BEFORE DOMES, SKYBOXES, artificial turf, sports agents, ESPN, and fantasy leagues, there was a game they usually played on grass. That game was football, and the men who played it were a special breed. They got their hands dirty. They would be pummeled, bruised, and injured, but continued to get up and hobble back to the huddle to take another snap.

Every week it was a different game in a different place, and these men were different from the rest of us. But while the game they played hasn't changed much over the years, the names of the players have.

Lem was one of those different men. Each Sunday in the fall and winter and once a year on Thanksgiving Day, he would suit up to do battle with valiant opponents while hoping and praying that he had prepared and was ready for game day. "I never asked the good Lord to win the game," Lem says. "But I did ask Him to let me play with the skill, talent, and attributes He had blessed me with. I asked Him to help me play the game with the true spirit of sportsmanship and to protect us from serious injury."

The night before each game, the Lions were subject to a strict routine to prepare for the next day. "In the evening, usually around 10:45 p.m., the coach would make his rounds, checking out every player and every room," Lem says. "It was very bad news for any absent player the coach discovered. There was an 11 o'clock curfew and lights-out at midnight. Everybody knew what the rules were, so we felt accountable for ourselves and our roommate."

Lem never broke curfew and always adhered to the rules. He'd grown accustomed to those sorts of rules growing up, and had no problems with this style of discipline.

On game day, Dr. Ira Echelan, a man of the church from Boca Raton, Florida, would make sure there was a minister or preacher associated with the league to provide chapel services. The chapel service would usually last about thirty minutes and be followed by the pregame meal consisting of just about anything a player requested.

"Most of the players would request a main course, including meat," Lem says, "but I realized early in my career that meat would stay on my stomach long after the game was over. I usually preferred a high carbohydrate meal of waffles and pancakes, bulking-up as long-distance runners would do." Lem firmly believes that a disciplined routine must be developed and maintained in order to make it in the league.

When he was on the road, Lem occasionally had a chance to enjoy Mississippi home cooking. "In Chicago, I would prefer to visit relatives for a home-cooked meal and pass on the local restaurants and nightlife," he says. "Rather than play around in the city, I wanted to rest and get myself mentally and spiritually prepared for the coming game. In many of the host cities, I would look up fellow Jacksonians (people from Jackson State) to share a few hours with."

Lem decided early in his career that he was not about to risk messing up his preparation for game day. "A player could be fined for other things, as well, such as being late for breakfast, lunch, dinner, team meetings, or missing flights," he says. "So I followed the rules. Besides, my dad always told me to show up 30 minutes before you had to be there." Lem always remembered that fatherly advice and carried it into the NFL with him. He was on time, every time, for every game.

One of his favorite places to be on time was Tiger Stadium. "When I was in Mississippi watching the Thanksgiving Day game, I would hear about Tiger Stadium and the great team that played there," he says. "As a result, in my rookie year when I first played there, it became a surreal experience, and I would not have been late for any reason."

Today, Lem cherishes the history and lore of that magical game of dreams, where he, Dick Allen, and a cast of thousands had played before. A place where, had they been allowed, horses and cows would have joyously been able to eat the lush green grass of Tiger Stadium.

"I've come to appreciate Tiger Stadium as not just a place where football players like Jim Brown, Bobby Layne and Gale Sayers once played," Lem says. "But I realized that some of the greatest baseball players in the Hall of Fame have also shared the field in Tiger Stadium—Ty Cobb, Hank Greenberg, Babe Ruth, and Hank Aaron. New turf and deluxe skyboxes cannot replace the memories or the spirit of days gone by and the great departed athletes who once graced our town."

In Lem's day, the single-most distracting issue was the discussion surrounding the use of artificial surfaces. Lem was not a fan of man-made playing surfaces, which promised to change the game. He preferred a natural surface. "The artificial turf at the Astrodome was terrible," Lem says. "It was very tough on the players' joints and knees."

As a result of those synthetic surfaces, Lem once suffered an extremely painful torn groin muscle against Houston. Late in a game inside the Astrodome, he went back to field a punt. "I was trying to evade several would-be tacklers," he says. "The last person I had to beat was Dan Pastorini, the quarterback and punter for the Oilers. As I moved quickly to my right, then back hard to the left trying to set Dan up, he hit me in mid-stride and I heard a loud pop." Sure enough, Lem had torn his groin muscle.

"But that was the nature of the job I had chosen," he says. "And every time I was hurt in my career, that spirit within me would say,

'Hey buddy, you're not hurt; go do your thing.' I played seven more games on Astroturf with that injury. That surface has contributed a great deal to destroying many professional careers."

Today, most indoor games are played on a new artificial surface called Field Turf. The Lions use it for all their home games at Ford Field in Detroit and in their practice facility in nearby Allen Park, Michigan. It has a lot more give to it, and it's infused with a crumb rubber infill from recycled car tires. In the last several years, it's made Astroturf and other similar surfaces obsolete.

Although Lem still prefers the real thing, he thinks that playing on Field Turf is a close second. "Field Turf is far more joint-friendly than Astroturf." Lem's favorite place to play the game is also the most joint-friendly stadium in the NFL—Green Bay's legendary Lambeau Field. "It had great natural grass and a heated coil beneath it to melt the snow," he says. "There were, however, many places on the field where the natural grass had been torn up by play."

Another stadium that Lem liked was Chicago's Soldier Field. "It was a nice park with a good playing surface," he says. "Another was the Los Angeles Coliseum, where I played my first four Pro Bowls. Dolphins Stadium was good, too, but Metropolitan Stadium in Minnesota was not so friendly. Most of the grass was gone when we played there. It was so cold when the Twins played, there was no grass left. Their solution was to paint the ground green."

Grass covered with snow had little impact on the All-Pro's psyche. "No, the cold never bothered me because I had mastered the 'mind over matter' philosophy," Lem says. "However, warm weather was truly my ally; I've always been a heat freak. I learned early that if your body doesn't mind the playing conditions, nothing else really matters. My body may have been cold, or too hot, but nevertheless, the game had to be played."

All the World's a Stage...So You Must Learn to Juggle

"To be or not to be—that is the question."
—Willie Shakespeare
"To intercept or not to intercept the script—that is the question"
—Key grip overheard on the set of "The Black Six"

IT WON'T BE ON ANYONE'S TOP 10-MOVIE list of all time. In fact, it would be surprising if it made any list at all. When you make a film like THE BLACK SIX, you're probably not expecting Academy Award nominations. But Lem had his reasons for making this "blaxploitation" film.

"The film project was done in the mid-Seventies," Lem says. I was approached by Gene Washington regarding a film that was being produced by the same man who had made DEEP THROAT. The film needed six black men for the leads, and Washington asked if Mercury Morris from the Dolphins, Carl Eller from the Vikings, Willie Lanier from the Chiefs, Joe Greene from the Steelers, and I would be interested in the parts. The six of us agreed. Four of the new film stars were also headed to the NFL Hall of Fame."

True, they were Hall of Famers, but actors? Well, that's another story. But just as Lem defended the end zone for the Lions, he defends the plot of THE BLACK SIX:

"It was a movie about a motorcycle gang," he says. "The country had been at war and the six of us had served in the military fighting overseas. We had signed a pact with each other, providing that if we survived, we would come back to the States, buy motorcycles, and just tour the country. The group's motto was 'Peace and Love, No Hassle.'"

Fortunately for Lem, he didn't give up his day job. But as a Lion, he did have a unique opportunity to witness first-hand the adventures of a writer who also decided to test the acting waters. Lem was not around when writer George Plimpton wrote his very original bestseller PAPER LION, which later served as the film template for the movie of the same name. The movie version of the book was filmed during Lem's rookie season. The plot was simple. A gangly and terribly feeble Plimpton would attempt to make the Detroit Lions at quarterback. It was reality TV nearly 40 years before its time.

Alan Alda was chosen to play the role of George Plimpton. "It was perfect casting," Lem says. "Neither Plimpton nor Alda were the most athletic guys. They were nice guys, just not great athletes." Lem also appeared in the film and remembers both men fondly.

"The whole team liked George," Lem says. "And most of us later attended the 40-year reunion of the production of PAPER LION at Ford Field (in 2003)." Many of the Lions captured in both the print and film depictions of the story were on hand.

Over the years, Plimpton kept in touch with many of the Lions and tried never to miss a game. Plimpton's favorite game-watching spot was at a place named the Blue Moon in New York City, where he and his friends witnessed the ongoing misery and woes of his team.

A Lions fan till the end, Plimpton died shortly after the reunion. Lem remembers the man who lived out his dream vicariously through others. "George was a good man, a bright man, and a man that will forever be a Detroit Lion," Lem says. "It was an honor to be there when we sent him off. Many of the Lions portrayed in the book and movie attended his funeral."

Turning to happier times, Lem thought back to PAPER LION. "It was a fun time," he says. "We were in camp and we were starring in a movie. It was a clear case of life imitating art, and art imitating life."

While Lem's role in the movie did not lead to a film career, he did pick up some pointers from a real Hollywood movie star. "I learned how to juggle," he says. "Yes, Alan Alda taught me how to juggle oranges. Alan wasn't very coordinated, but he did teach me how to juggle. I still can do it today."

Footprints IV
Fame's rain

He was not a young man now. Nor was he an old man. He was merely a man. A man who had attained a trunk full of rewards, awards, and treasures on earth. He was a man who, for the most part, was content with his station in life. And for good reason. He had made it. He had reached the point in his life where one can look back with pride at one's accomplishments, yet still look forward with the hope of accomplishing more.

On this part of his journey, there were many options still open to him. There were many roads, with many forks in them that he could take. And as he came to each fork in the road, the man always relied on his instincts, his guts, and his faith to take him down the righteous path. That he could always count on and pray for—this guidance from above.

He never let him down. He never forsook him. He never led him down the wrong path. His direction was his direction, ever since, well ever since he was a little boy. And he knew it, believed it, cherished it, and worshipped this relationship with the Lord.

The young man was never too shy, too proud, or too big to ask directions from the great mapmaker. He knew deep in his heart that no matter what, He would oversee and keep a close eye on all the journeys that he set out on.

The man forgot one thing, however, as he traveled this part of the journey. For a few moments, and it was only for a few brief moments that the man forgot to take Him on the journey. The man believed that he could find his way on his own. He did not need a map or the mapmaker. He could do it on his own now. After all, look at all he had accomplished. Look at all he had achieved. Look how far he had come since that day on the beach when he was a little boy and he ran against the wind.

The man now felt that he could do it alone, and why not? His accomplishments were great and people told him so. Some people told him over and over, complimenting him almost to the point of exhaustion.

And the man listened. And he believed in what they were telling him. Soon His voice could no longer be heard. Now he heard many voices telling him this and asking him that. And the man listened to them all. The man was lost.

Soon, the man would be on the road again. But now he did not know which way to go. Up ahead, there was a fork in the road. And up above, storm clouds were brewing. The man started to sweat. Storms never bothered him before, but that was before. Now he was alone, alone with only his thoughts, his ego and his foolish pride.

"I can find my way back."

"I know I can."

"I don't need any help," the man said as he looked nervously at the dark clouds that had gathered.

Just as the man came to the fork along his path, he veered to the left down a dark, dreary road. It was then that the rains came. Not in buckets, but in stadiums filled with water. It was water that Noah could relate to and water that washed over the man.

The man did all he could do to take cover under a barren oak tree that had seen better days. He huddled at the base of the oak and watched it rain and rain and rain. The man just sat there and watched it rain for what seemed like days. And as he did, the tears flowed from his heart through his eyes. As he watched, the green grass faded to mud.

It saddened him. The man dropped to his knees in the mud and he began to pray.

"Lord, I can't see the beautiful grass."

"Lord, please help me."

"Lord, help me, I'm lost."

Slowly the rain began to let up.

In an instant, it stopped completely.

The man was soaked. But he did not care.

The man was covered in mud. But he did not care.

The man stared at the ground and at the muddy earth. Then ever so slowly, he lifted his head. The mist of the hard rain covered him. The man smiled. Slowly he rose to his feet.

On his way up, he noticed some sweet basil on the ground.

He picked a stem and held it to his nose.

Lem's mother, Berdell, and his father, Lem Sr., provided a strong foundation and were a great inspiration.

The Stardells, featuring Lem on drums, at 33rd Avenue High School in Gulfport, 1960.

Lem in his infancy, circa 1946.

Jacci's mother, Sadie Ballard.

Jacci's great grandfather, Major Head.

Jacci's grandmother Dora Head.

Lem shows off his backpedaling technique at Jackson State.

In 1962, Lem (Number 10) played quarterback for 33rd Avenue High School in Gulfport, Mississippi.

Lem picks off a pass against Grambling.

Rehearsing the Mexican hat dance at Jackson State University with Lottie Campbell in 1965.

Getting some reps in at quarterback for Jackson State in 1964.

In 1967, Lem and Lions teammate Mel Farr, respectively, were named defensive and offensive NFL rookies of the year.

Lem and Paul Naumoff mug for the camera.

Lem had 8 interceptions averaged 21.2 yards per punt return in 1969.

After Dick "Night Train" Lane retired, Lem had big shoes to fill in Detroit.

Photo Courtesy of Kirt Doke

The gridiron gladiator in his heyday.

Photo Courtesy of Kirt Doke

Even while on the sidelines, Lem always kept his head in the game.

Lem looking "superfly"
in the early 1970s.

Lem, along with Mercury Morris,
Gene Washington, and Mean Joe
Greene, played a motorcycle outlaw
in 1974's The Black Six.

Lem, ever stylish, shows off
on the links in the offseason.

Lem gets ready in the locker room
to celebrate a Lions victory.

Clinton Jones, Lem, and Tom
Dempsey tour in the Orient during
a U.S. Department of Defense
tour in the early '70s.

It seemed the longer Lem played, the more facial hair he added.

(Clockwise from top left) Tom Dempsey, Bob Lilly, Ernie Wright, and Lem head to the Pacific Islands to visit U.S. troops on a 31-day tour in the early '70s.

Lem with Pistons forward George Trapp and Lions fullback Lawrence Gaines in the mid-1970s.

Lem with Lions quarterback Bill Munson in 1969.

Lem relishes the moment with teammate Jim David's son Peter.

Lem and Mike Weger feel the pain of another loss to the Vikings in 1973.

Lem sports the classic two-bar facemask of the 1960s.

Lem runs agility drills during training camp in the early '70s.

Earl McCullough and Lem led the Lions to a 10-4 record in 1970.

An open-field takedown of Chicago's Brian Piccolo.

The 1967 defensive rookie of the year shares a moment with teammate Pat Studstill.

Lem and linebacker Paul Naumoff at Lions training camp, circa 1968.

Getting ready to pick off another pass.

Lem receives an award in Chicago from Mike Powell for his charity work with the Better Boys.

Lem confounds the 49ers special teams as he returns a punt against them in San Francisco.

Neither rain nor mud could stop Lem from intercepting Vikings quarterback Fran Tarkenton.

Lem and Lions safety Mike Weger prepare to shut down a screen pass.

Even with a cast on his broken right wrist, Lem was still capable of picking off an errant pass.

Lem dared opposing quarterbacks to throw the ball in his direction.

Lem defends his home turf.

Lem's catlike reflexes and great lateral movement kept opposing receivers on edge.

The Supernatural kept his opponents guessing about a corner blitz.

Lem always relished a battle against the Cleveland Browns.

Long before Mel Gray and Eddie Drummond, Lem was the Lions' premier punt returner.

Lem and the Lions had a distinct home-field advantage at old Tiger Stadium.

Here, Lem does his best Barry Sanders impression.

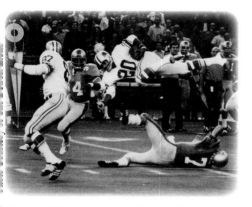

Houston Oilers quarterback Dan Pastorini (No. 7) upends Lem after he notched another interception.

When it came to defending his end zone, Lem was king of the jungle.

Lem's bust in the Michigan Sports Hall of Fame.

Lem is proudly inducted to the Pro Football Hall of Fame in 1992.

Lem with his presenter, Jimmy David, basks in the glow on induction day in Canton.

Lem (left) serves as a Lions honorary captain in 2004, with Eddie Drummond (18), Stockar McDougle (73), and Fernando Bryant (25).

Jacci Barney's favorite photo of her husband, taken in 2000.

Pistons great Dave Bing, basketball coach Bill Frieder, and Lem.

Lem is ordained as a minister
by Pastor Ronald G. Arthur at
Springhill Missionary Baptist
Church in Detroit.

Lem is in high demand as an
inspirational speaker.

Lions offensive lineman Damien
Woody, left, attends church with Lem.

Lions cornerback Dre' Bly
joins Lem at church.

Pastor Nicholas Hood III and
Lem before church service.
Lem gave the sermon that day.

Celebrating Christmas
at home in Michigan.

From left to right, sports agent Del Reddy, publisher
Michael Reddy, Lem, and author Gus Mollasis discuss
the making of The Supernatural.

Detroit's Trilogy of Number
20s: From left to right, Billy
Sims, Lem Barney, and Barry
Sanders.

Lem donates an all-weather Detroit Lions jacket to the Michigan
Historical Museum.

CBS football analyst Marcus
Allen interviews Lem at the
Pontiac Silverdome in 2001.

Lem and Earl Fisher at Detroit's
Tiger Stadium in the late '90s.

ESPN's Chris Berman and Lem
are all smiles at Ford Field.

August of 1999 with former Rams
greats Eric Dickerson and Jackie
Slater at a Pro Football Hall of Fame
function

At Ford Field for Detroit's tribute to the
Local Initiatives Support Corporation. From
left, Detroit Mayor Kwame Kilpatrick, Lem,
and former Lion Robert Porcher.

A Davenport University function, where Lem is a member
of the board. Pictured with Pittsburgh Steelers great and
Fox sportscaster Terry Bradshaw.

Lem with former Lions offensive lineman John Gordy.

Mel Farr and Abe Thompson in Chicago at Mel's annual Christmas party.

Lem and comedian Tom Arnold pose for a photo at Tiger Stadium in the late '90s.

Lem and former Lions great Alex Karras mug for the camera.

Lem with Denver Broncos star cornerback Champ Bailey.

Hall of Fame cornerbacks Mel Renfro, Kenny Houston, and Lem.

Fearsome Foursome defensive tackle Roger Brown joins Lem for the 35-year reunion of Paper Lion in 2003.

Lem shares a moment with a sure-fire Hall of Famer—Washington Redskins cornerback Darrell Green.

Working the stage with Marcus Allen and the band at Ronnie Lott's children's charity.

Lem shares a moment with Lions owner William Clay Ford at Ford's induction into the Michigan Sports Hall of Fame in 2005.

Former Pro Football Hall of Fame president John Bankert, left, with Lem, Barry Sanders, and Billy Sims.

Lem shares a moment with Hall of Famer Roosevelt Brown's son.

Billy Sims, Thom Seafron, Barry Sanders, Lem, and fraternity brothers at a Football Hall of Fame function.

Lem, Oscar Robertson, and Dick Barnett attend Dave Bing's induction into the Basketball Hall of Fame in Springfield, Massachusetts.

Lem, right, at Dave Bing's induction to the Basketball Hall of Fame with Earl Harvey and Oscar Robertson

Wounded Lion

"Amazing Grace! How sweet the sound
"That saved a wretch like me.
"I once was lost, but now I'm found,
"Was blind, but now I see."
—*John Newton, 1725-1807*

$\mathcal{T}$HE DARK DETROIT STREETS WERE adorned, if that is the right word, with skid row bums, drug dealers, and prostitutes. In a page torn from a travel log of places that one could most likely go to lose their soul, this was ground zero. It was here where dreams died, if they ever dared to be dreamt at all. That's the way it was on the mean streets of Motown. When you lost your way, you usually ended up here, stranded at the crossroads of despair and delusion. It didn't matter who you were or who you knew, if you booked this trip, you were assured of having a hell of a time. Even the rats that slithered down the ally knew that.

At the rear of the place that even Detroit cops were too afraid and too smart to enter, the man with the derby made his appearance. Lem Barney snuck into a darkened doorway and through the shadows looking to fulfill a desire. As he entered this hellhole, he tuned into one of the subjects the voices on the jukebox were speaking of. It came from a time that had passed him by. He knew the song and he knew the singers.

It was Dennis Edwards and the Temptations. "I'm doing fine … on Cloud Nine," came the refrain. Lem slid into a back booth and handed the man with the red shirt a hundred-dollar bill. In return, he was handed a bag.

Just that quickly, the transaction was completed. Quickly, nervously, Lem grabbed his derby and headed for the door. The man behind the bar, who looked tougher than a dozen defensive linemen, eyed Lem as he headed out for the long ride home. As Lem's big Lincoln pulled away from the joint, his radio was playing. It again was the Temptations.

"I love the Temptations," Lem thought. "Papa was a rolling stone …wherever he laid his hat was his home…"

For Lem at this point in his life, the Temptations were not a group he wanted to hear, see, or feel. And they were definitely not something he wanted to give into. But in reality, he knew that temptations would always be there in his life, just as they're in everyone's life, lurking around every corner, waiting for the person to let their guard down, weaken, and give in to them.

"Temptations for some come in the form of greed, fame, money, gambling, drink, women and/or drugs," Lem says. "The devil provides a temptation for everyone and knows what flavor you like. Temptation is always lingering out there. That's why you must always be prayerful and maintain a dialogue with the Lord."

For years, this dialogue between Lem and the Lord was as clear as a Nat King Cole vocal and as smooth Eddie Kendricks and the Tempts singing "Just My Imagination." Lem and the Lord talked daily. He was obedient. This loyal and humble servant talked with Him and prayed to Him. And then it happened. A crack in his coverage and the Lord's message was picked off by the horned one, like a wobbly pass by a second-string quarterback to a rookie receiver running a poor route.

"For years, I never touched the stuff," Lem says of drugs. "I was always aware that it was around. I was around people using it, but was never tempted to join in." Temptation was knocking on his door, though. And while he had seen this temptress before and had turned down her overtures many times, he felt his resolve weakening. The rationalizations began.

"Well, what's it going to hurt?"

"If I just have a little, it won't hook me."

"Who's going to know?"

"Who's going to care?"

"Just a little and I'll be cool."

"Yeah, I'll fit in."

He heard all the voices except two—his own and His voice from above. He was no longer on Cloud Nine. His head was now merely cloudy. Lem, a man who prided himself on being able to resist temptation, now faced the cold hard truth. He no longer held his head high. Now he hung it down ashamed. He had always been high on life, the Lord, or love, but now he was high on something else—grass. And where before he was high just to run on it, now he needed it to fly. The Supernatural had become Super Fly.

"You know, if you stay around something long enough, eventually it will get you," Lem says. "It was tough. I had sunk to a depth I could not see myself climbing out of. I had let myself and so many others down. For well over seven years in the NFL, I had not given in to those temptations. First I tried marijuana. Then it became cocaine."

Lem blames no one but himself. "It was my decision," he says. "I made that decision. Drugs became like air for me, easy to get everywhere—and no one was immune. Drugs touched all facets of society and all classes of people."

For a long time, Lem could see the temptations that lurked around every corner. "I was strong enough to say no—and mean no—for a long time," he says. "For years, I thought drugs would be a hellacious ride, but as time passed and I witnessed people using them with no apparent negative result, my will weakened. A little at first, until you get to a level where you don't want to give up that good feeling, still believing you can quit anytime you wanted."

In the beginning, Lem used drugs only during the offseason and only at home. But eventually, it reached a point where he was doing it often and would go anywhere to get it.

Lem paints a picture of those places, where the canvas of his life was devoid of any and all light. It was now filled with only one hue—darkness. "There was no night too dark to prevent me from fulfilling the temptation that had taken over my soul," he says. "No distance too far to travel, no price too high to pay. My teammates had become people who would kill and be killed, people whose minds and hearts belonged to the darkness. I know how I got there, but I wonder how God brought me out of it, saved me from those places, these very treacherous places."

Lem looks back on it and cringes. "I thank God for His deliverance from it," he says. "The use of drugs takes a person to the point where they lie to others and lie to themselves to protect their soul from reality. It was a part of my life that I certainly am not proud of. The darkness of my situation worsened when the knowledge of my weakness became public knowledge."

Those were the dark times when a Lions All-Pro and Hall of Famer became little more than a wounded lion on the prowl. "I had let down my family, my teammates, my friends, my church, and the people who I had helped overcome these same temptations," Lem says. "I had become a hypocrite. These terrible things still come back to haunt my mind. Those were my wounded years, the wounded times."

Through the grace of God, Lem was able to start the healing process that would finally deliver him from darkness. "I had become severely depressed and finally realized that I could not get out of this situation without God's help. My weakness had been revealed, but in acknowledging that weakness, I was helped and the wounds began to heal."

But the trauma of these experiences and a continuing battle with temptation, made Lem realize that he needed to share his pain and shame with somebody to help him through it. "That somebody was Pastor Moss—James Everett Moss, one of the greatest men I have ever come to know, who came to my side when I needed him." Moss' spiritual and psychological counseling helped Lem endure these traumatic times, but it is Lem's faith that carried him through.

"I had lost hope," Lem says, "but not my faith."

In the face of the highest obstacles, Lem believes that people must maintain their faithfulness and do what He asks us to do. "When I was using drugs," he says, "I wanted to fast-forward my life right out of the problem. I would go through the trials, turmoil, crying and weeping continually. But it is at these times that you cannot lose your faith. With continual prayer, hope is restored. The Lord can deliver me through this. I would tell myself, 'stay hopeful, faithful, and prayerful.'"

Lem's friend Benny White remembers the tough times Lem faced. "I felt he was going through what he needed to in order to realize who God intended him to be," White says. "I didn't feel sorry for him. He didn't feel sorry for himself. He was aware of the things he had done and what they had done to him. He understood more than anybody that he had to go through what he was going through."

Lem believes that if we are to grow as people, that we must all suffer at times. "It teaches us stick-to-itiveness," he says. "People are always being tested, and even God will test our faith from time to time. God wants to see how strong our faith is."

Lem points toward the scriptures as his safe harbor. "The stories in the scriptures are applicable to our lives and our illnesses," he says. "The things the scriptures relate provide lessons on how we can turn our lives around in the face of adversity. We must remember that He has that power."

Lem believes that people have to believe, especially when they drift into the darkness. "They may feel there is no light at the end of the tunnel," he says. "I know. I've been there. That's the reason reading the Bible is such strong medicine for the heart and the soul. The Bible guides me through the tough times."

Tough times are something that Lem knows all too well. "Tough times do not last, but tough people do," he says. "Though I walked through the valley of the shadow of death … the point is that you go through it—and don't get stuck."

Lem stresses that when you're down on your luck, you should not feel alone, and that temptation has been around longer than the Lions have gone without winning a championship. "Recall that Adam was tempted with the forbidden fruit," he says. "That's why God wants us to have our faith in Him, trust Him, and to do the things that we know are right. It's a sad commentary when a person doesn't recognize right from wrong. There will always be those situations when the evil one will bring you just what you wished for. But it's up to us to say no."

There are times, he says, when you have to walk away—and mean it. "To know that if you look at it, it can capture you. Temptation is always there, but He is always with us. Our Creator and Master has always provided us with a way to escape temptation. We must trust in Him and know what is right and what is wrong."

Lem cites the ultimate example of overcoming temptation. "In forty days and forty nights, Jesus was tempted. And every time the horned one threw a temptation at our Lord, he overcame it. It is written, and it is important to memorize scripture. It helps us claim victory over Satan and it helps us win others to Christ."

Lem knows from his own experiences that overcoming temptation can be very difficult. "You must really want to do it," he says. "Whether a person is a gambler or thief, if you want to rid yourself of it, He will deliver you from it."

Jerry Green remembers the tough times Lem went through. Lem had come from humble beginnings, but in Detroit, he became friendly with a wide range of people in show business and other arenas. "As a Detroit Lions star," Green says, "Lem also traveled extensively and had often visited California and Hollywood. Some of that glitter was bound to rub off. I was disappointed in him."

"There was a great deal of pressure," Lem says. "Teammates, neighbors, people who worked in grocery stores—they all tried to involve me in things I should not have been involved in. I managed to avoid drugs for seven years, but being around so many people constantly urging me to join in, eventually succeeded in pushing me over the line."

Lem believes it was the grace of the Lord that brought him through this dark period in his life. Even while he was telling himself that he needed to stop, his prayers were not sincere. And the Lord knew. "Following public disclosure of my weakness and the shame of letting down all of the good people who supported me, a big wound was created in my soul. I realized at that moment that I had to be sincere and up front with the Lord. The Lord knows our hearts. By my sincere prayer for deliverance, that prayer was answered, and I've never looked back."

With his moral vision restored, Lem recalls those dark days and tempting times by counseling those in similar situations today. Based on what he's learned from that experience, Lem is now using his celebrity and fame to help kids overcome some of the same temptations he faced.

"You have to say no and really mean it," he says. "Associate yourself with only those who support your principles. And don't put yourself in harm's way. Avoid situations where temptations and the promoters of temptation try to seduce your better judgment."

Lem's friend and former teammate Mike Weger remembers how Lem went through his tunnel of darkness, knowing that only Lem could change himself. "If you're going to change, it must come from inside," Weger says. "And that's where Lem's strength was from the beginning. It was beautiful to see that he didn't lose sight of what made him who he was. It was his internal strength."

Lem knows there's only one way to get through the highs and lows of life. "Surrender to the Lord," he says. "Not most of it, or some of it, or a lot of it, but all of it. I had to surrender it all to Him." His struggle with drugs was a terrible price to pay for a lesson in principle, but having gone through it has made him a better person. "Now I'm better able to help others who may also be trapped in the same darkness."

Today, Lem's days and nights are filled with light, as he remembers a time when there was only darkness and despair.

"I'm doing fine…up here on Cloud Nine."

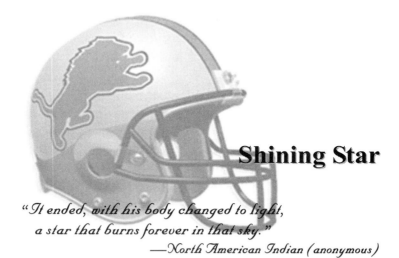

Shining Star

"It ended, with his body changed to light,
a star that burns forever in that sky."
—*North American Indian (anonymous)*

$\mathcal{I}$T WAS NATURAL FOR LEM BARNEY TO play the role of superstar. Frequent visits to the Pro Bowl helped write a football résumé that was being polished for Hall of Fame consideration. "While I was playing, I never thought of statistics," he says. "I never thought about how many yards I gained, or how many interceptions I made. I only thought about one thing each and every day I played. And that was preparing myself to give the best effort I could in order for our team to have a chance to win."

That's why Lem took practice so seriously, for it is on the practice field that your most basic skills are honed and polished. "It's not possible for any player to just show up on Sunday and expect to perform at their best," Lem says. "At least I couldn't."

Lem's work ethic and practice ritual helped him become the best football player he could be. And Lem became an NFL superstar. Under the public spotlight, Lem always displayed that star quality. He was flamboyant and walked with a swagger. Muhammad Ali once said, "It's not bragging if you can do it." And Lem Barney could do it.

And though he was a star, he never really acted like one. While he dressed a little flashy and perhaps invented "bling bling" long before hip-hop, Lem was one star you could touch. The common man, as well as the celebrity, felt an affinity with him. Sure, he hung out with other stars, but this star belonged to the entire galaxy that made up his solar system.

Lem's world includes everybody. And because of that, his star shines just as brightly with the big and successful as it does with the little guy. That is his appeal and what has kept him in the sights of sports fans in Michigan for all these years. When they go out stargazing, Lem is easy to spot. He's the one in the derby, with the bright smile and the twinkle in his eye.

Lem's son, Lem III, remembers when he first realized his dad's star quality. "My parents were very open-minded," he says. "During Motown's height, my mom and dad got married on Christmas Eve 1962. That anniversary was always a big time for all of us. They would have an anniversary party every Christmas Eve and everyone was invited—Marvin Gaye, Smokey Robinson, Dave Bing, Mel Farr, and many others."

"Mel and I had just been drafted," Bing says, "and I was completing my rookie year with the Pistons when we met. We very quickly became close friends. We were young, thinking we could conquer the world, and we did our best to make that dream a reality."

And while he forged a bond with Farr, Bing says he didn't know much about the other Lions rookie in 1967. "I didn't know who Lem Barney was," he says. "But over time, I got to know him as a person and a great football player. He has that personality that makes it impossible to dislike him. He's loving and engaging and giving. And as a friend, you can depend on Lem. He is, in fact, like a brother to me."

Bing remembers when his friend's star fell. "It was painful for me because we were so close and I had never seen him in a condition like that," he says. "I saw Lem struggling with the problems and tried to help him deal with it. Instead of worrying about his career and what the public thought, I was just trying to help him be safe."

Lem's turnaround left a lasting impression on Bing. "I will remember Lem for his remarkable abilities as football player," he says. "I'll remember him as having a great heart. And I'll remember him because I've never met anyone who would say anything negative about him. He's the kind of person you want to be around. He has that affect on people."

Lem was at ease in all situations, especially at home during one of their anniversary celebrations. "Those parties were pretty exciting," Bing says. "Lem and his first wife, Martha, were fun people to be around. They enjoyed life to the fullest and that was the reason so many people wanted to be a part of their lives." They didn't think of each other as stars, but instead just as people. "As we got older," Bing says, "we would reflect with much pleasure on the memories of those parties. Many other well-known people were supportive of Lem, as well. We've all moved on in life, but the foundation of our friendship has remained solid."

Jim Acho knew Lem from a different perspective—that of a starstruck fan and co-worker at Mel Farr's Ford dealership. "When I first met him, I was shocked by his down-to-earth presence," Acho says. "He was, after all, an All-Pro and a Hall of Famer. But he was also very approachable. A homeless person on the street could approach Lem and be treated like an equal."

Bill Cosby, one of the true kings of comedy, considers Lem his friend. "I met Cosby during my rookie year during the 1967 Pro Bowl in Los Angeles," Lem says. "CBS was hosting a banquet that week and many celebrity hosts from current television shows were on hand to act as guides for the players in town. Cosby was my host, and our relationship bloomed quickly. Within just a few moments, I felt I had known him all of my life. He was even so gracious as to invite me to stay with him at his home."

At various parties at Cosby's house, Lem met people like Anthony Quinn and Jack Lemmon. And he still keeps a close relationship with "The Coz" today. "Bill's appeal to audiences of all persuasions is based on his humor and humanity. He's able to mix with anyone. Adding to his charisma is the fact that he's a scholar, an educator, a great comedian, and an athlete. He loves and enjoys people—all people—and he doesn't care what color they happen to be."

Like his friend Cosby, Lem is also a man who loves people and treats everyone equally. Willie Farmer, Lem's high school band teacher from his 33rd Avenue High School days, knew Lem well before his star had risen. "Lem is about the most genuine, down-to-earth man I ever knew," Farmer says. "He's an athlete, a gentleman, and a scholar." Farmer appreciates Lem's sense of humor, too.

In 1971, Farmer was named as a delegate to the 88th National Education Convention. Lem offered him a ride home from the airport upon his return, and Farmer accepted. When his plane landed, Lem showed up, as scheduled, in his Lincoln Continental. But he was not alone. "With him were Bob Lanier and Dave Bing of the Pistons," Farmer says. "As I was climbing into the car, several onlookers at the airport…gathered for a look at me."

Farmer couldn't understand what all the fuss was about. That's because the joke was on him. "Lem, Bing, and Lanier," he says with a laugh, "had told the crowd that I was the new arriving ambassador from Ghana."

Celebrity or not, Lem's star has always shone brightly at home. His sister Varina Carter can attest to that. "My mother and father would be so proud today if they knew just how close we have remained," she says. "My sister has even erected a shrine to Lem at our Gulfport family home as a show of respect for our mother's lifelong admiration of her son."

While Lem was in Detroit becoming a star, his mother started a professional scrapbook for him, as well as a memento wall filled with his trophies and testimonials. "Every Thanksgiving, Lem would bring home new trophies for the wall," Varina says. "Even after he left the pros, he would come home with more mementos. And every highlight of his life, from high school to the pros, my mother kept on her wall or in a scrapbook."

Lem is still a celebrity in his hometown of Gulfport, Mississippi, and each time he returns home, he always makes the rounds to keep in touch with his old friends.

A Starr Remembers a Star...

The dark night was filled with stars glistening brightly. They seemed to fill the black sky with anticipation. Two men, one already a star and the other wishing to become one, quietly scanned the heavens for some sign of what was to come on the eve of the 1967 NFL season in Green Bay, Wisconsin.

Bart Starr, quarterback of the defending NFL champion Green Bay Packers, and rookie cornerback Lem Barney of the Detroit Lions, envisioned the day ahead. Starr was planning to continue carving his name in the record books, while Barney was hoping his destiny might be the same. The two had a date with history, squaring off against each other for the first time. Their paths would cross many times over the ensuing years—both on and off the football field.

Starr remembers the man who would become his friend and who would become a star in his own right. "Over the years, Lem Barney and I developed a deep mutual respect," he says. "I knew going into that first ballgame that he was a very talented...player. We reviewed and studied his game films, and there had never been any question within our organization that Lem was a fierce competitor—a very smart and outstanding opponent."

Lem reminded Starr of his teammate and fellow Hall of Famer Herb Adderley. "They were both outstanding cornerbacks," Starr says. "It's rare that in one division, you get two corners who were as good as those two were. I thought Lem was uniquely smart. He had great quickness, and his anticipation was exceptional. It's interesting because, obviously, as a quarterback, I tried not to have the cornerback read my eyes. With Lem, that was hard to pull off. He was outstanding mentally and physically."

The three of them were always at their best come turkey day. "I always looked forward to playing the traditional Thanksgiving game against the Lions because of the rivalry," Starr says. "We had immense respect for the Lions. It created a special time for us during the season."

Bart Starr and Lem Barney were two stars with a tremendous gift—a mutual love for the game and for each other, armed with an ability to harness a great attitude and take life in stride, no matter what was thrown their way. "Lem is my friend," Starr says. "He's a super gentleman ... someone you'd love to have as a teammate."

According to Starr, talent like Lem's comes from the heavens. "One of the first things that you try to teach anyone," he says, "is that most talent is God-given. Granted, some receive more than others. But I think that God balances that by giving all of us the capacity to manifest an outstanding attitude. I believe that word— **attitude**—along with **love**, are the two most powerful words in our vocabulary."

Starr believes that if an athlete's attitude is as it should be, then he can manifest that talent to a high level. "I think, then, what you do with that attitude is that you recognize that you have to work to surround yourself with outstanding individuals. Yes, you have to play together as a team, but I think equally important is that you have to be able to take a look inside and see what's inside of you [for] a kind of courage and mental toughness, innate goodness, those types of things."

Starr, like all Hall of Famers, was able to make the necessary sacrifices to succeed in his career. These men understand organization and preparation—and they all have that burning desire for excellence. "That has to be what drives you," he says. "We need to seek to excel—not just be satisfied to be good, because we have the capacity to be better than just good. Our spirituality is where we wear it. Not talking it, but walking it. When you genuinely feel that commitment, then you live it."

Starr and his teammates knew, too, that a large part of their success could be attributed to their coach, Vince Lombardi. "Leadership begins at the top," Starr says. "That's what changed when Coach Lombardi came to the Packers.

Unfortunately, the situation in Detroit was not quite the same. Throughout most of Lem's eleven seasons with the Lions, the team was unable to put together a winning game plan. "It was more difficult for Lem to get into the Hall of Fame than it was for other players with winning organizations," Starr says. "But I do feel that people look at individual talent and how it contributes to the success *of the entire team. And when you look at individual talent, Lem Barney was a shoo-in for the Hall of Fame."*

Although Starr himself is a legendary Hall of Fame quarterback and Super Bowl MVP, that doesn't necessarily define him as a human being. "I'd like to be remembered as someone who had a respect for his God and his family," he says. "Hopefully, I made the best use of my God-given talent and that I was a friend."

Starr takes inspiration from Stephen Covey's book THE 7 HABITS OF HIGHLY EFFECTIVE PEOPLE: "I want to live the life of integrity and make a difference in the lives of others," he says. "And to me, that's exactly what Jesus did."

Not surprisingly it's also what these two stars, named Starr and Barney did on and off the field. Now many years removed from the bright lights of the game they loved to play, they still shine as brightly as ever. And because of their integrity in the game of life, these two stars will always be worthy of being looked up to.

Time to Leave the Pride

"In the jungle—the mighty jungle, The lion sleeps tonight."
—*G. Weiss, H. Perretti, L. Creatore*

THEY SAT TOGETHER AT THE AIRPORT. Two friends—two football players and two All-Pros, having lunch and conversation.

"I'm finished," Lem said.

"Finished? What do you mean?" asked Dallas Cowboys guard Rayfield Wright, who had just played as Lem's teammate in the Pro Bowl.

"I mean I'm done playing football. Done with the game," Lem said.

"What are you talking about?" Wright asked. "You still have five or six good years left."

"Yes, and that's where those years are going to stay," Lem replied. "In me."

It was 1978 and a few months earlier, Lions coach Monte Clark had advised Lem that perhaps he might want to consider retiring, or perhaps pursue a trade. Clark felt that the Lions needed restructuring and that Lem might want to look elsewhere. That conversation led Lem to examine his conscience, his career, and his life.

"I thanked him," Lem says. "I thought 'this may well be the best time to leave football.' And when I left, I was determined that I wouldn't try to come back later like so many others had. When I went into Clark's office that day and had that conversation, I resolved that that was the end."

Lem was hanging up his spikes. Not because he couldn't fly up and down the field anymore, but because he just didn't want to go through the motions. He was tired and had nothing left to give the game. His body was still willing, but mentally, he felt that he had nothing left.

His retirement in many ways is similar to that of the great Barry Sanders, who inherited Lem's Number 20 with Detroit in 1989 and who left the Lions rather mysteriously to retire after the 1998 season, still with many years of potentially great football left in his career.

"I relate to Barry," Lem says. "Yes, he may have gotten tired of the game, but perhaps the game had lost its challenge for him. He could have played more, just as I could have. But we had both resolved to retire."

Lem came to his decision much quicker than Sanders did. "I mulled it over during the offseason and left the game without regrets whatsoever," he says. "I resolved that after the Pro Bowl, I was going to leave the game."

In the last game of the 1977 season at the Pontiac Silverdome, Lem and the Lions once again battled the Vikings. In what turned out to be his final game as a professional, he intercepted yet another pass. Then after playing in his seventh and final Pro Bowl, Lem called it quits. He couldn't lie to himself or to others. The thrill was gone.

Back then, as he does today, Mike O'Hara covered the Lions for THE DETROIT NEWS. It was his first year on the beat—and Lem's last in the league. "Lem's play in that last year was excellent," O'Hara says. "His primary assignments were moved around a bit, and in one game near the middle of the season, he took a hit to his thigh." Lem's agility was somewhat limited over the last half of the year, and the Lions used him sparingly thereafter. "While his skills may have diminished a bit," O'Hara says, "his spirit of aggressive and committed play still remained."

Nonetheless, O'Hara understands Lem's decision to walk away. "Eleven years at the top in the NFL in that day was a good long career," he says. "How much he had left I really don't know, but I know that Lem enjoyed the lights, enjoyed the people, and enjoyed having a good time."

"What the general public didn't know was that Lem got up early every morning and read his Bible and lived his beliefs." O'Hara saw it all firsthand. "What else is there that anyone can ask of a man?" he asks.

Today, the man who looks like he could still lace 'em up is content with his decision to leave the game. "I was able to leave without becoming physically, spiritually, or mentally damaged—and I felt good about that." Lem says. "However, I was a bit surprised that I didn't miss the game very much after leaving."

Media Darling

"This is Howard Cosell . . . yesterday the Detroit Lions beat the Bears on a spectacular interception by the great Lem Barney . . . from tiny Jackson State."

—*Monday Night Football*

WHILE THE FANS LOVED HIM AND THE players respected him, it was the media that truly recognized Lem's supernatural abilities. And it was Jerry Green who christened Lem with the nickname "Supernatural."

Recognized by the best in the business, Lem remembers the often imitated but never duplicated Howard Cosell. "Cosell was the premier telecaster of all sports," Lem says. "He had a great insight into sports and players. His sportscasting career lasted so long because he did it right. Cosell didn't care what people thought about him because he knew his own strengths."

In 1992, as Lem prepared for his induction into the Pro Football Hall of Fame, he called Cosell to invite him. But Cosell was suffering from cancer and was unable to make the trip. He died in 1995 at the age of 77. Still, Lem remains thankful for all the accolades Cosell showered him with on the air. "In reviewing other plays and players, Cosell would compare the action to the way I would've done it. I'll never forget the introduction Cosell would offer when I was involved."

Mis-tah Lem Bah-nee from tiny Jack-son State! Cosell would say in his inimitable staccato.

"I adored and admired Cosell for his true professional work. He was so good to me. On his Monday Night Football halftime highlights, he would show replays of the Lions game often focusing on a particular cornerback. It gave me and the entire team excellent national exposure."

"And the pass is picked off...by the great Lem Bah-nee...from ty-nee Jack-son State!"

Frank Gifford shared the booth with Cosell on many a Monday night.

"The world and ABC got to know Lem Barney on Monday nights," Gifford says. "Lem was very colorful and always seemed to have a few words for everyone he passed. While the Lions did not often share the Monday Night Football spotlight, Lem still managed to have a couple of great Monday nights for us. I also recall the Pro Bowls he played in where he stood out."

Another pro announcer Lem admired was Van Patrick, who covered the Lions in Detroit. "Van was like Howard and broadcast our games very well," Lem says. "He had a good voice and was a man respected by everybody in town."

Lem also spent some time in the broadcast booth himself. "My early years allowed me to work with Ray Lane and Charlie Neil," he says. "Because of my background in the game, I tried to point out the nuances of the game, things people didn't see or understand."

Lem always tried to let listeners know there were other things to look at besides the ball carrier. "It's natural to focus on the ball carrier," he says, "but there's much more to a football play than that. Much on the field happens before a person even gets the ball. Usually, that's the most important action."

Lem did broadcasts mainly of Southwestern Athletic Conference games. He also did work with BET. "At this point," Lem says, "I've been involved in television or broadcasting on and off for about 26 years, and I plan on continuing as long as I enjoy it."

Lem finds that the work behind the microphone gives him a different thrill than playing the game. "As a ballplayer, I was always striving to be a big-game player and accomplish exciting things," he says. "Success on the field provided me with nice recognition from the public. My teammates would provide the pat on the back in support of my efforts. Based on that experience, as I broadcast games today, I try to bring the same level of excitement to the listeners and the crowd."

Lem says that the media have always been fair and kind to him. "I've tried to always return that level of respect and courtesy," he says. "Having played the game, I'm less likely to be critical and more likely to offer objective analysis."

Perhaps in this way, Lem may have matched the master, Howard Cosell—the man with the bad toupee, distinctive voice, quick wit, and a seemingly inexhaustible vocabulary.

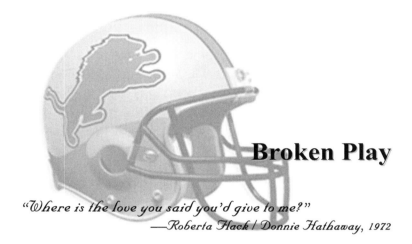

Broken Play

"Where is the love you said you'd give to me?"
—*Roberta Flack / Donnie Hathaway, 1972*

$\mathcal{T}$HEY STARTED OUT IN HIGH SCHOOL as sweethearts, in love, committed, and on their way to the chapel for an everlasting "till death do us part" union. Only somewhere along the way, something broke. Lem and Martha Barney decided to go their separate ways.

"We were married on December 24, 1967, at the end of my rookie year and just before the Pro Bowl," Lem says. "Year one of my career with the Lions was a tremendous success. I graduated from Jackson State and was drafted by the Detroit Lions. I had a great rookie season and then married my college sweetheart. I had a military obligation following college and went into the Naval Reserves. It was an exciting, tumultuous time for us."

Quickly, Lem's tone turns melancholy as he recalls the end of the romance. "Martha and I were divorced in 1999, following thirty-two years of marriage. We had reached a point … where Martha didn't want to be married any longer, and the romance left our relationship." Lem hoped that they could work things out, but it simply wasn't meant to be. He reflects on the lost time and the lost love. "It was a pivotal point in my life," he says.

"While I was studying for ordination, I met Jacci. It was during this crucial time in my life that I fell head over heels in love with her and shortly after we said our *I do's*."

Lem credits his faith for helping him get through this painful time. His life was turning around with a new love, but it was also a time for reflection. "It hurt quite a bit," he says, "because it was more than just the two of us going our separate ways. We also had to consider the kids. Lem III was in college, and Latrece was about to start her career in music. It was tough, but I thought that it would be better for all the parties involved to get it over with as soon as possible."

As a dedicated family man, the breakup weighed heavily on Lem. "It was hard for the kids at times, but I think over the years, the wounds have healed. Martha and I had a great relationship, and we still maintain contact from time to time. I don't think either of us harbors any ill feelings as a result of the divorce. I still pray for her."

Knowing firsthand how a marriage can fail, Lem has formed some definite opinions of what young couples should do before they tie the knot. "Before I agree to perform a ceremony," he says, "I require the couple to consent to pre-marriage counseling for two months. A marriage is more than just love. It's a lifetime of commitment based on honor, respect, and trust. In my opinion, counseling is important—and perhaps even vital—to a happy and successful relationship between a man and woman."

Lem also believes it's important to receive counseling from a man of the cloth because the important lessons about marriage derived from the Bible are explained to the happy couple. "These lessons are a very important part of a decision to spend the rest of your life with someone," he says.

Lem is well-qualified on all fronts to talk about this subject. From the pulpit and from the pit of pain and self-doubt, Lem worked his way through his tough times. "There were times when I had to wade through self doubts," he says. "But since I found Jacci, I have found a new life. Jacci is a spirit-filled lady solidly in my corner who encourages me, motivates me, and inspires me. We are kindred spirits committed to prayer and sharing in the gospel of the Lord."

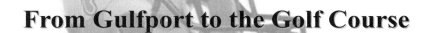

From Gulfport to the Golf Course

"And Tiger Woods becomes the first African-American to win the Masters and wear the green jacket."

LIKE MANY BLACK KIDS GROWING UP in the 1950s, Lem Barney was unfamiliar with golf. It was a game he believed that only people of privilege could participate in. He'd never been exposed to it. Little black kids from Gulfport, Mississippi, just weren't seen on the local courses. But in years to come, golf would become another love in his life.

"My introduction to golf began when I was invited by a friend to join him working as a caddy in Gulfport," Lem explains. "As the home of several large and important military bases, there were many golf courses in the area that were always looking for kids to carry bags for paying guests." But any idea he might've had about learning the game himself was out of the question. He was an African-American kid and was not allowed to play golf in Mississippi. But for Lem, being a caddy and earning a few extra dollars, learning the game, and seeing more of life would be just fine.

"I caddied to earn spending money and managed to develop a pretty good understanding of the game, the clubs, and the techniques," he says. "Golf was a prestigious and expensive proposition. Initially, beyond the mechanics, I didn't particularly care enough about golf to pursue it."

Early in Lem's time at Jackson State, a remarkable black athlete named Lee Elder was making a name for himself on the PGA tour. His golfing skills were the talk of African-American neighborhoods across the county. Back then, a black golfer was very unusual, a rarity on the PGA tour, and unheard of in the Gulfport area. But Lem and Elder's paths would cross in a way that would mean more than any caddy fee or any pro-am appearance.

In Lem's second year with the Lions, golf would once more become a subject of some interest. "During this time, some of my teammates were taking to the links and enjoying some success," he says. "But my involvement in that sport was limited to watching my teammates' homes while they flew off to play in celebrity tournaments." After seeing his friends get invited to tournaments around the county, he couldn't understand how they could afford to be flying off to play golf. Their response surprised Lem. "Yes, they said, golf was expensive, but most often, celebrity golf tournaments and classics had sponsors who would pay your expenses."

With his eyes now open to this new opportunity, Lem hustled down to the local department store in 1969 and purchased his first starter set of golf clubs. The price? A hundred dollars. "I took the clubs to the driving range and just banged away, trying to duplicate the techniques I'd seen as a caddy," he says. "Eventually, I managed to figure things out. But a large problem with being self-taught is that things I learned early on became the bad habits I had to overcome later." Lem continued to work on his game over the years, getting lessons from pros and friends.

Today, he has a seven handicap and considers himself a good golfer. "Golf is a game that duplicates life," he says. "The gentleman's game provides nearly unlimited opportunities to bend the rules or to improve your score. Perhaps the game is best described as a contest between your body and your conscience. For that reason, it's a game that not only demands skill, but personal character as well.

Shakespeare wrote, "To thy own self be true," and to no other man can you be false. This quote captures the essence of the game and forms the basis of golf's great personal satisfaction, as well as its great personal aggravation. "There's an expression that my friends and I frequently use to illustrate the philosophy of the game," Lem says. "If you find that your ball has landed on a lily pad, hit it quickly before it falls into the water."

Lem sees some parallels between golf and football. "In both sports, you have to prepare both physically and mentally," he says. "And in my life, I've found that preparation is the one facet of competition that's absolutely necessary. In the game of golf, it's a story of proper alignment, movement, and assignment of available tools and knowing what you need to accomplish with the next play."

Of course, Lem brings his faith onto the golf course and has since the 1970s, when he first tried to master the game. "There are intangibles that go with faith," he says, "but if you believe in the Lord, you will learn that with Him, you can master anything."

Golf brought Lem more than just sporting enjoyment. In the early 1970s, he began accepting invitations to play in celebrity golf tournaments around the country. A few years later, during one of those outings, Lem had the good fortune of meeting Lee Elder. Elder had been one of Lem's golf role models—a black man making it to the top in what had been a white man's game.

"Lee Elder is a classy guy with a fluid swing that makes the game look deceivingly easy," Lem says. "But I was soon to learn that class was not something limited only to Lee in that family. There was a young lady at that event named Jacci Ballard, who also had a lot of class and immediately caught my eye." It turned out that Jacci was Elder's sister-in-law. One thing led to another, and after marrying Jacci in 1999, Lem became related to his golf hero, Lee Elder.

Following the little white ball around the fairways of America has afforded Lem the chance to meet some of the biggest and brightest stars of all time. Among others, Lem has played in the Bob Hope, Andy Williams, and Dinah Shore celebrity golf tournaments. At these, he's met many great people, including members of the several professional sports halls of fame.

Paul Krause is a fellow warrior who played against Lem on the football field, as well as on the golf course. He credits golf with cultivating an important friendship. "In the early years, Lem and I played a lot of golf in Grand Blanc, Michigan," he says. "The game provided us with friendly competition that carried over onto the football field. Both on and off the football field and golf course, Lem developed into a very good friend and remains so still."

Hall of Fame receiver Bobby Mitchell hosted his own tournament that Lem regularly took part in. "Lem is one of the guys who we always expected to be at or near the top of the list of winners," Mitchell says. "He has an excellent game, a low handicap, and people always want to play with him. He was one of the best players, ranking right up there with other excellent golfers from other sports."

Lem's enthusiasm for the game of golf is evident. If the invitation to play is in the mail, all it needs is the time and the place, and there's a good chance that Number 20 will go tee it up.

"The greatest tournament I ever participated in was the American Airlines Golf Classic," Lem says. "I've played with Bill Freehan, Jason Thompson, Al Kaline, and Brooks Robinson. That tournament is nicknamed the Rolls Royce of celebrity tournaments. "American Airlines flew us all over the country," Lem says. "They gave us sportcoats, shirts, ties, and golf shoes. Then we were scheduled to play golf with top CEOs of Fortune 500 companies from around America. An invitation to this celebrity tournament was almost worth the torn groin muscle I received many years ago."

Another great tournament for Lem was the Don Drysdale Hall of Fame Classic in Palm Springs, California in the 1990s. "I played with Don for five years in that outing until he passed away," Lem says. "The thing that made Don's one of the best was the fact that only Hall of Famers were invited to participate." From golf, tennis, horse racing, auto racing, baseball, football, basketball, and hockey, Hall of Famers were everywhere. "We played for prize money, and the CEOs played for trophies," Lem says. "I had the opportunity to play with people like Juan Marichal, Yogi Berra, Joe Namath, Joe DiMaggio, Otto Graham, Reggie Jackson, Willie Mays, Ernie Banks, Lou Piniella, Paul Warfield, and Deacon Jones. These were former athletic greats from all over the country—people you'd never be able to meet and socialize with without these great tournaments."

Lem's humility, gratitude, and "aw, shucks" attitude are part of his charm. The little boy in Lem lives on in the person of Lem the Hall of Famer. And it is this sense of wonder that makes him so approachable. As he approaches greats from varied walks of life, Lem does so with a purpose, taking nothing for granted. He simply meets and greets them all the same way, with a warm genuine smile. And the feeling that he exudes, the feeling you get when you meet him, is supernatural.

"Golf is a great game played by great people," Lem says. "Spending three to four hours on a golf course with friends provides you with a chance to get out of doors, breathe fresh air, share immediate success and failure, and get to know people better." And Lem has gotten to know some of the greats on the gold course, including Willie Mays, and Joe Dumars.

An afternoon of hitting a ball down God's green fairway while playing with some of the greats of all time. Sharing memories and making new ones as the sun sets and the putts sink. Not a bad way for a former caddy from a small Mississippi town to spend the day.

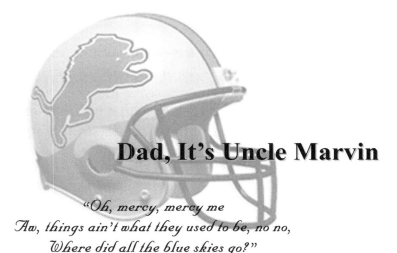

Dad, It's Uncle Marvin

"Oh, mercy, mercy me
Aw, things ain't what they used to be, no no,
Where did all the blue skies go?"

—*Marvin Gaye*

$\mathcal{T}$HE TWO FRIENDS WERE SMILING. THEY were just hanging out together on a beautiful spring day, listening to tunes on the radio and reminiscing about the good old days. And they had a host of good old days they could recall at the drop of a derby.

Ever since training camp in 1967, they'd been close. Mel and Lem. Lem and Mel. The two would be asked to lace up their athletic shoes and use their God-given talents to take Detroit to the Promised Land, far away from the many years of losing and the tumultuous riot-torn streets of that violent summer.

That was a lot to ask of any two great athletes, let alone two rookies. But it was a challenge that Lem and Mel Farr accepted without reservation. "We were close right away," Lem says. "We understood each other right from the beginning. We were really close friends and spent a lot of years together."

In that first year, they both made history, as Lem won the Defensive Rookie of the Year award, and Farr won Offensive Rookie of the Year. That's an accomplishment that has never been achieved before or since in NFL history. "We were awfully proud of that," Lem says. "Awfully proud. We were on the opposite sides of the ball, but we were on the same team. We were trying to do our best and win one for the city, win one for our coach, and for each other. We never got there, but it was not from a lack of trying. It was just not in the cards for us to win it all back then."

For many years, that same tune played on for the Lions players, coaches, and fans alike. A sorrowful song of loss, composed with a full orchestra of violins, sour notes, and enough blues to make B.B. King, king of the Lions. On this day, however, only the sounds of sweet music filled the carefree air of 1984. Lem and Mel tooled around listening to tunes, smiling, laughing, and remembering. It was a glorious Michigan day that cries for the car top to be down and the tunes on the radio to be turned up. Having just finished a tennis match, the two friends smiled, basked in the sunshine, and counted their blessings as they mouthed the words of the songs that they knew by heart that were being blasted on the car radio.

"Ain't nothing like the real thing, baby"
"Ain't nothing like the real thing."

The two former All-Pros were in rare form. Sitting side-by-side on beautiful spring day, Farr in the driver's seat and Lem riding shotgun, they took a stroll down memory lane with the sweet sounds of their friend Marvin Gaye providing the background music.

"I ain't got time to think about money
Or what it can buy…"

Song after song played on the radio. Then the musical medley would start up again.

The car ride ended as Farr turned the corner and headed into his driveway. As the car pulled in, he spotted his son running to meet them. He was visibly upset. "What is it, son?" Farr asked.

"It's Uncle Marvin, Dad. He's been shot … he's dead!"

Stunned, Farr hugged his son and then with a startled look on his face, he hugged Lem. The ride was over. The music had died. Neither Lem nor Mel will ever forget that day and the circumstances surrounding the death of Marvin Gaye. And so ended their relationship with the man with perhaps the sweetest voice in the history of soul music—of any music.

"He was outgoing, giving, and so sharing and so caring," Lem says. "And he just loved children." And Gaye demonstrated that on his *What's Going On* album, with the song "Save the Children."

"That's why the children's song is on there," Lem says. 'Who really cares?' Marvin cared. He loved them and cared for them in the hope of tomorrow. He will be remembered forever. And his music will live on."

Farr remembers Gaye as someone who desperately wanted to live out his athletic dreams. "We befriended Marvin and Smokey Robinson," Farr says. "Marvin started coming out to watch us play football. He really wanted to be a football player. We encouraged him to work out and told him we'd get him a tryout."

Gaye began lifting weights and running two to three miles a day. "He was serious about it," Farr says. "He wasn't doing drugs or alcohol…and we encouraged him so much."

Mel dispels a Motown myth about the recording, "What's Going On." Many have said that Gaye made a trade with his two friends, telling them that if they got him a tryout with the Lions, then he'd put them on the record. "The deal of trying out was a separate entity," Mel says. "He just wanted us to sing back up on the album."

Mel remembers the day Marvin died. "I was with Lem, listening to Marvin," he says. "We had just finished playing tennis. Lem and I were discussing Marvin and our concern for the public image he was presenting in concert. Some of the things he was doing were in very poor taste, and we agreed that he needed a new routine. We feared for his career. To this day, I don't really know and I'm not going to speculate on what happened," he says.

Lem still can't understand the senseless tragedy. "Marvin and his mom were in one of the rooms talking, when Marvin's father came into the room," Lem says. "Marvin asked his father if he would leave the room while he and his mother were talking."

Reportedly, the exchange between Gaye and his father became more heated. Marvin's father retreated to an upstairs bedroom, retrieved a handgun, and at point-blank range, fired two bullets into his son.

It was April Fool's Day 1984.

The great Marvin Gaye was dead, one day shy of his 45th birthday.

Brother, brother, brother
There's far too many of you dying
You know we've got to find a way
To bring some lovin' here today
Father, father
We don't need to escalate
You see, war is not the answer
For only love can conquer hate
You know we've got to find a way
To bring some lovin' here today

Singing his friend's song took Lem back to another time and place, when he and Mel rode around town, basking in the golden age of Motown.

As that spring day came to an end, deejays across America spun the sweet sounds of the man from Motown. People of all races, creeds, and colors sat and listened to the music that broke down barriers and professed hope for a better world. Music that connected people instead of dividing them; music that was not exclusionary, but that instead included everyone. Music that touched the senses, fed the soul, and moved mountains. These were the pure sounds of a genius taken before his time.

Along with the rest of the country, Lem Barney and Mel Farr, two of Marvin Gaye's dearest friends, wept silently and wondered aloud…

C'mon, talk to me
So you can see
Oh, what's going on
Yeah, what's going on?
Ah, what's going on?

Of Used Cars and New Testaments

"Just $99 down and $99 a month drives it away."
—Used-car TV commercial starring Mel Farr

𝒯HIS COMMERCIAL, AND OTHERS JUST like it, bombarded Detroit television airwaves back in the 1980s and '90s, featuring Mel Farr, "Superstar car dealer." During that time, Lem, the Supernatural, was making his own headlines:

5/16/93—Barney Criticizes Report:

DETROIT (UPI)—Detroit Lions legend Lem Barney, facing two counts of drug possession, claims the charges against him are untrue and prosecutors have portrayed him "like some kind of Jeffrey Dahmer."

Barney refused to discuss details of his March 19 arrest, but said authorities "have tried to turn a matchstick into a dynamite stick. This so-called incident is a non-story. I'm not a Jeff Dahmer. I'm just a man who's active in his community and church." Barney's problems began on March 19, when Michigan State Police discovered the Hall of Fame cornerback's car crashed into a Detroit freeway guardrail. Police said they found marijuana "roaches" and cocaine on the floor. Barney, who is active in children's anti-drug programs, also had a blood-alcohol level of 0.108, higher than the legal limit, police said.

If convicted, he faces up to four years in prison. His trial date has not been scheduled. Barney, of suburban Southfield, played 11 seasons with the Lions, rising to stardom after being drafted as a little-known defensive back from Jackson State University in Mississippi.

There was nothing supernatural or positive about these headlines for Lem. It seemed that his star was falling. And Farr could sense it. The man with the sure hands, the quick feet, and the uncanny ability to get himself out of traffic jams on the football field now found his world crashing down on him.

At the time, Lem had been working for fourteen years as a public affairs specialist for a gas company. And his arrest on drug charges was also very public. "I was forced off the highway and ran up on a guardrail," Lem says. "When the police arrived, they searched my car and found half of a joint. Based on that, they wanted to claim that I also had crack cocaine in my car. I did not." The gas company, always concerned about its public image, fired Lem, even before a trial on the charges had been conducted. But the evidence supported him and he was found not guilty.

"At the time, I was disappointed," Lem says, "but I understood the corporate community. I realized that they didn't want negative publicity, but I loved the job. It was people-oriented, and I love to inspire, motivate, and encourage people. At the gas company, I did various sporting programs with students and senior citizens, as well." Lem got great satisfaction from his job. But he believes that if people don't grow, or if they choose to live with negative feelings, life is much more difficult. So this event ended another chapter in his life, and it was time to move on.

The next chapter in Lem's life involved an old friend, and it began just down the street at the corner of Greenfield and Nine Mile on a used car lot. "After I left the gas company, Mel called me," Lem says. So it was on to Mel Farr Ford in Oak Park, Michigan.

"Mel called and asked if I wanted to get into the car business," Lem says.

"It might turn out to be something that you really love," Farr told him.

Lem agreed. "I started my new job in 1993 or 1994. It was a job that was people-related and something I felt I could do with integrity." Over time, Lem became a finance manager for seven years. "There were some aspects of the car-selling business that were unattractive," he says. "I understood that it was a business, and sometimes operating a business can be difficult." Lem appreciated Farr's help in his time of need, and he encouraged Farr to reach for the stars.

"I tried to encourage him," Lem says, "and that chance arrived when I worked at his headquarters. It was a personal joy for me to be associated with him again while he was building his automotive sales business." Lem eventually moved from finance into auto sales his last few years with Mel. "That position gave me more free time and an even better opportunity to work with people," he says. "During my years with Mel, I enjoyed watching him work at what he liked to do best. And one of the things he enjoyed was starring in his own television commercials. Mel and a camera always made a great combination."

For Farr, the decision to bring Lem into the fold was a natural. "A friend in need is a friend indeed," Farr says. "If a friend is down, you need to lift him up. Our relationship was like brothers. If your brother is down, you do what you have to help lift him. Lem was a financial manager, involved in new car sales, and did some public relations work for us. He was just a good guy and I enjoyed our time in business together."

Jim Acho, a metro Detroit attorney who represents Lem and many other retired NFL and MLB players, worked at Mel Farr Ford. "Lem was the most upbeat person I ever knew," Acho says. "He was always providing encouragement and motivation. He took me under his wing and watched out for me. He tried to do little things to help bolster my sales and my spirits."

Acho learned many lessons on the car lot from Lem, lessons you can't pick up in a sales meeting. "He taught me to treat everybody equally," Acho says. "I've seen him in every type of arena and he would talk to Lloyd Carr and Nick Saban the same way he would talk with an unemployed person looking for work. He treated everyone with respect and love." Acho says he wishes he could be as humble and gracious with people everyday as Lem is. "He's not afraid to live the way that Christ taught us."

Treating people well is Lem Barney's specialty. After leaving Farr's dealership, Lem had a lot to offer the world. After he was ordained and thinking of entering the ministry, Lem became area director of The Fellowship of Christian Athletes in 2000. "When that opportunity presented itself, I jumped at it," he says. "It was great to be part of something that I had been involved in for over 50 years.

The FCA was wonderful for Lem and it gave him a real lift. He also worked to lift others. "I preached the teaching and principles of Jesus, and it was the right position for me at the time," he says. In January of 2004, Lem left his position at the FCA to explore other opportunities.

With each new chapter in life, Lem remains upbeat and maintains a positive attitude and work ethic. "I've never spent time at a job doing something that I didn't really like," he says. "I've always tried to push myself forward and engage in work that was important to me."

Footprints V
On the Right Road

The man was back on track. His wisdom accompanied him and comforted him like a warm blanket, a good fire and better company on a cold winter's night. He took great joy, not so much in the goal, but more so in the journey of doing, or trying to do, especially for others. It filled him, fulfilled him and warmed his heart as he reached out to many of his brothers and sisters who'd fallen by the side of the road.

The man had become a wise man. He had grasped two very important concepts. Now he knew that you truly get by giving. And he also knew that people truly don't care what you know, until they know that you care.

This man gave much, cared much, and knew much. Most importantly, he shared much with everyone the wisdom he received by following Him.

He shared His words with young and old.

He shared His hope with those who were wounded or well in spirit.

He shared His peace with Black and White.

He shared His love with Man and Woman.

He shared His faith with believer and nonbeliever.

But above all he shared all that He above had shared with him.

And in doing so it made him feel good.

Yes, you truly get by giving.

The man felt good, because after all, he was a good man.

A good man—not a perfect man, but a good man—a man of God who did Godly things.

He covered his fellow brother and sister in a cloak of words and prayers and went wherever he was needed. Wherever the Lord wanted him to go, he went.

His discipleship was faithful.

His discipleship was steadfast.

His discipleship was devoted.

His discipleship was true.

And the Lord knew it.

So the Lord called him often.

The man always listened.

His discipleship was tuned in to his voice.

When he was asked to go and serve, he served.

He did not ask, "Why Lord?"

He did not ask, "Where Lord?"

He merely went to serve the Lord.

And the Lord was pleased.

It pleased the man to please the Lord, so that's what he did.

The man served the Lord in both word and deed.

He served the Lord, not just on Sundays and not just on some days, but in all the days of his life.

In small ways, big ways, humble ways, and sometimes it seemed, in supernatural ways. But through it all, the long days, the short days, the hot days, and the cold days, he served the Lord.

Through the years and through the joy and tears, he served the Lord. Through the sunny days and the days that the storms came, he served the Lord. Through the days when he walked tall and when he fell to his knees, he served the Lord.

And because the Lord was pleased, the man was pleased.

He smiled with a joy at the heavens with a contented heart.

The night was clear and the stars in the galaxy seemed to smile and wink back at him.

All was right in the man's world.

He knew it and The Lord knew it.

He was back on the right track.

Bride

"There is no fear in love;
But perfect love casts out fear."

—*John 4:18*

𝒯HE SUBJECT OF MARRIAGE CAME UP AS Lem spoke to his friend who had suffered through a divorce. Lem's friend wondered if there was someone out there for him that was perfectly suited as a love match. "The Lord will hand-pick someone for you," Lem told him. "You won't meet her in a bar or on the dance floor; you'll see her in a pew on Sunday morning.

Then Lem flashes a smile and says grace. When guests are preparing to dine with Lem and Jacci, every meal starts off with a prayer. It doesn't matter if the meal is at a local restaurant, a black tie formal event, or at home.

You can always rely on the Barneys for words of thanks before the meal. At home, Lem enjoys the culinary mastery of his wife and partner. "Jacci's an excellent cook," says Lem, who knows about great cooks. He grew up with two of them. Now I have my own home version of Emeril Lagasse, thanks to the skills and love of Jacci."

Lem has found a mate he feels was handpicked for him. "She's the closest thing to my mother, Berdell," he says. Lem and Jacci were married April 10, 1999, and it's been the perfect union ever since.

"When we wake, we greet each other with a kiss and an 'I love you today and always,'" Lem says. "Then there's praise to the Lord."

Jacci is usually at home at the computer, setting up administrative appointments for her husband. "She also has a real passion for the kitchen," Lem says. "When I come home, we'll have a nice dinner and reflect on the day, and talk about plans and family things. After that, we're ready to retire. Before we sleep, it's another kiss. 'Goodnight, I love you, sleep well, and be an angel.'"

Their secret for a happy union is simple—center your lives on God. "Marriage is ordained by the Lord," Lem says. "Two shall become of one flesh, and that is the mystery of the Lord, and we do all things to the glory of God."

Lem believes another essential element to a successful marriage is compromise. "We cannot go to bed mad," he says. "We try to resolve all of our infrequent differences before retiring. I could possibly be wrong or you might possibly be wrong. We put it on the table and work on it again."

The love Lem feels for his bride is evident in his words and deeds. "What makes Jacci so special is that she's so focused and blessed with her God-given talents, skills, and attributes," he says. "There's nothing she can't do. She is loving, compassionate, and simply the best. She fills our home with joy and asks for nothing in return. She's thoughtful and reaches out to people. We have a little saying: 'All that I would be to others, a cheering ray of light, inspiring them with courage to climb to newfound heights, I would be to you.' So we know that the human spirit soars with hope when it is led by the church and the Word, and we are right there together. The Lord expects us to do that."

When counseling couples who're planning on marriage, Lem offers simple scriptural advice. "Go over scripture-inspired messages for two to three months," he says. "Marriage was ordained by God and He says, 'For thus shall a man leave his father and his mother and take on a bride and the two shall become one. This is the mystery of marriage.'"

Lem learned a lot about a successful marriage from his mom. "She would say, 'The same thing you did to get this woman, you have to do to keep this woman. Don't let the sizzle fizzle.' My mother also taught me that you have to be a gentleman with your wife, and make her your best friend."

Lem and Jacci first met on the golf course in 1987 at Hilton Head, South Carolina. "The second year Lem attended, I met him," Jacci says. "I had been busy producing the fashion show for the tournament, and I didn't know who Lem Barney was. So I asked my friends."

The second year at the tournament, they crossed paths at a Red Roof Inn where the program's models were staying. "Lem says he saw me the first year he attended, but I didn't speak to him. As soon as we met, we both felt the magic. After that first meeting, we spent four days together and I felt a special spark." Now in their seventh year of marriage, Jacci says that her honeymoon has been spent moving into their new house.

While it is a house filled with many of her husband's trophies, it is also a house filled with love, joy, and the spirit of the Lord. Jacci says that's what brought these two together most.

"The important thing about Lem is that he's a perfect gentleman, always loving, caring," Jacci says. "And he truly loves the Lord. I had always dreamt of marrying my knight in shining armor, and God answered my prayers—He sent me Lemuel Barney II, the man of my dreams, the man I had always prayed He would send me."

Jacci Barney was born in Washington, D.C, to devout Christian parents. "My grandmother was very strict, but she loved the Lord and her family," she says. "Mother spoiled me, but I always respected them both and loved them dearly. I miss them and think of them often. I thank them daily for continued guidance, direction, education, and the love that I have for the Lord and my fellow man."

Her grandparents, parents, and two older brothers have gone to glory, she says. But she still has three beautiful sisters: Millie, Rose ("Rosebud"), and Dara the Great, as well as a handsome brother, Bob. "I have an array of nieces and nephews that complete our happy family and that love each other unconditionally."

"Married life is a joy. We put Christ first in our lives and everything else just works together for the good because we put our trust in Him," she says. "When we get up in the morning, we worship and praise the Lord... Having been taught by our wonderful pastor, Ronald G. Arthur, we must stay prayerful all day."

Like most couples, the Barneys do not always agree, but they've learned to pray on all things and never let the sun go down without working the problem out. "God can fix everything," Lem says. "We can only mess them up."

As far as the demands of celebrity, Jacci is a seasoned pro. "I met Lem after his football career," she says. "Celebrity functions are just another event for me. I've been on the celebrity scene since elementary school. My former brother-in-law was Lee Elder, the first black player to play at The Masters in Augusta. My sister Rose, who was married to Lee, produced an annual celebrity golf event for almost 30 years. We worked with celebrities like Bob Hope, Michael Jordan, Bill Russell, Serena and Venus Williams, Johnny Mathis, and many others."

When the guys get together for an outing or other event, it's old hat for Jacci Barney. "I'm not one for the limelight," she says. "Lem loves everyone and everyone loves Lem. I'm fine with that. His best quality as a man is that he loves the Lord. Lem is a genuinely loving and caring person and he is always concerned about other people's needs. If he's ever upset, you'll never know. As he says, He takes it to the Lord and leaves it with Him, and He will make it right."

Jacci sees her husband as a role model that she not only genuinely loves, but who also inspires her. "Lem has given me tremendous strength and inspiration in my faith walk with Christ," she says. "He constantly reminds me not to worry about anything, but in all things pray. Turn it over to the Lord and He will work it out according to His will. Lem is a good man, a genuine friend, and a wonderful nurturing father and granddad."

It's obvious to everyone that Jacci has found her match in Lem. "He always tells me I'm the closest thing to his mom," she says. "And I feel as though he knew my mom just like I feel I knew his mom— even though we've never met. When Lem and I got married, my sisters and brother were present. They said, 'I am sure our moms and grandmothers are up there in heaven rejoicing.'"

During the ceremony, when Jacci was asked if she would accept Lem as her husband, before she had a chance to reply, all of her sisters said, "We do."

"My family loves Lem. Our faith is the glue cementing this union, which I feel was ordained by God. God really has the ability to not only give you what you need, but He will give you what you want. God gives you what and who He feels is right for you, provided that you let God make the decision."

According to Lem's sisters, their family feels the same fondness for Jacci. "Jacci is so good for Lem and he loves her dearly," Lemelda says. "She's just a great, sweet person and they're a very good family.

"They needed each other," Varina says, "and I'm glad she was sent to him when he needed her most.

For the Barneys, home life is simple, spiritual, and it's where they connect. "We're basically homebodies," Jacci says, "although we travel quite frequently. Lem can cook, but I do most of the cooking. That's my passion—cooking and decorating. Lem loves chicken wings. We enjoy the comfort of our home. We get great joy in inviting others to fellowship, to enjoy great cuisine, and create loving and cherished memories."

While there may not be a trophy in their cabinet that declares it, it's obvious that these two prize each other more than anything else. When Jacci thinks of the thing first engraved in her heart about her husband, the message is sweet and spiritual: "I will love him always for his laughter, his love, generosity, and foremost, his love of the Lord," she says.

Before It Was Cool—Stylin'

"Fashions fade; style is eternal."

—Yves Saint Laurent

To SOME HE WAS FLASHY, AND TO others flamboyant. To some, a hot dog and to others a Coney Island with heavy chili and mustard. To some, the Supernatural, to others Super Fly.

On this point everyone can agree.

Lem Barney is warm to everyone.

And because of that warmth, Lem Barney is cool.

No matter what your impression of Lem Barney, one thing is certain. He impresses you one way or another. It may appear that he grabs the spotlight in a loud and almost brash way, but at the same time, a thread of humility always runs through Lem's soul. And that suits him just fine, better than an Armani jacket and custom derby from Louis the Hatter.

Long before it was fashionable to be fashionable, Lem was in fashion. Lem was cool. He doesn't follow trends; he creates them. Someone once said that you can't teach a person to be cool—and they were right. But if anyone could give a class in being cool, and do it in a classy way, it would be Lem Barney. This humble man with small town, God-fearing values and a smiling swagger, could give Broadway Joe Namath a run for his money in the cool department. In a word, it's style. Either you have it or you don't. And Lem has it.

So what makes up this cool man's ensemble? Well it's a combination of things. While it's been said that clothes make the man, it's also true that Lem makes his clothes. Let's start with that famous derby that tops off the Lem look. Was there anyone that looked better in a derby? Charlie Chaplin or maybe Patrick Macnee? But let those guys try to cover Charlie Joiner or Don Maynard one-on-one and look cool doing it.

Over the years, fans weren't the only ones to take notice of Lem's unique fashion sense. His teammates certainly did. Often, they would smile and shake their heads. Clear evidence they didn't understand "the 'look," but they went along with Lem for the ride. In a tribute to "The Derbied One," some 47 of his Lions teammates accompanied Lem down to Canton, Ohio, all sporting derbies in his honor at his Hall of Fame induction ceremony in 1992.

It's not known whether their bus was fashioned after one of the psychedelic VW's from the '60s, but one thing is for sure—all of Lem's teammates were a little cooler for having made the trip with him. Scout Will Robinson, one of the people responsible for Lem coming to the Lions, remembers Lem before his sense of style had evolved.

"Lem probably doesn't remember, but I recall a time when he didn't own a suit," Robinson says. "As we were preparing for that first press conference following his signing, we had to take him to a department store downtown to buy one."

As for developing his very fashionable look, Lem remembers buying clothes off the rack and the times his suits were custom-made. He credits his early upbringing as being the roots for his wanting to look good, especially for church. Strangely, it's Lem's mom who's partially responsible for bringing Lem's "derby look" to the masses.

"The derby is a by-product of something I saw on TV," Lem says. "I was a Fedora hat-lover, and in the second year I moved to Detroit, I used to wear Adams and Stetsons from college. Once I was in the NFL, I sent my mom to London on a vacation. She had a great time there, since she was also an art and nature lover." While she was there, she called and asked Lem what he wanted from London.

"I told her that the only thing I wanted was an English black derby."

She not only brought back a black derby, but also a gray and a brown derby. Ever since, Lem has worn derbies. "I liked the derby because I enjoyed television shows about super investigators—shows like The Avengers. Wearing a derby just appealed to me and seemed cool. Even today, when I dress up, I wear the derby."

Rounding out the rest of the "Lem look" was easy. You could find him shopping with some of his teammates on the streets of Detroit and, naturally, looking pretty dapper whether browsing or buying. "In the 1960s in Detroit I shopped at Harry Cousins and Louis the Hatter," Lem says. "I bought my first few suits from Louis on Woodward; I lived right around the corner then."

Lem remembers a time before large chain stores, mega marts and discount stores, where local specialty stores prided themselves on both quality clothes and hand-tailoring purchases for each customer. "At the Hatter, players would always receive nice treatment from excellent salesmen," Lem says. "A suit complements a man, especially the man who works out and maintains a good physique. And that store knew how to tailor a suit."

Among the Lions, Lem definitely raised the bar when it came to fashion sense. "Lem was a year ahead of me," former teammate Charlie Sanders says. "Earl McCullough and I came into the NFL at the same time as rookies. Mel and Lem were the team fashion trendsetters." One of the first things Sanders realized about Lem was that if you weren't dressed properly, you couldn't hang around with him. "In order to be associated with Lem, you'd have to go out and buy a whole new wardrobe," he says. "It cost the rookies a lot of money to develop and maintain a friendship with Lem. He wasn't derogatory—he just liked his fashions."

Lem demonstrated the same level of persistence in converting a teammate into a fashion plate as he did in preventing a first down. "If he was critical in a joking manner, he was not going to let up on you until you changed," Sanders says.

Sanders remembers the versatility of Lem's ensemble. "He had an outstanding wardrobe, and we never saw him in the same suit twice," Sanders says. "In terms of fashion, Lem always dressed to the nines."

He maintained that habit after retiring from the game, and it's something he has in common with his wife. "Jacci really dresses nice, too," Lem says. "She wears all of the latest fashions. She has a real fashion sense and a tremendous figure. We're very complimentary to each other." Seeing his wife attired in her Sunday—or Wednesday—best, for that matter, can leave old Number 20 speechless. "She takes my breath away," he says.

Where, before, Lem's mom picked out derbies in England and brought them across the ocean for her son, today Jacci picks out clothes in Canada and brings them across the river for Lem. "For the last four years, I've been doing commercials for Freed's of Windsor, and we've been spending a lot of time there," Lem says. "It's Jacci who does the shopping. She picks out the suits, ties, and everything. I totally trust her."

Roles of a Lifetime—Role Player

"In the creative process, there is the father, the author of the play; the mother, the actor pregnant with the part; and the child, the role to be born."

—*Konstantin Stanislavski*

LEM HAS PLAYED THEM ALL. THEY ARE his roles of lifetime. "As the family's only son, when I wrote to Mom and Dad from college, my salutation would be, 'Love, your favorite son,'" Lem says.

"I never ever wanted to do anything that would bring shame or dishonor to my parents. They trained me to have respect and reverence for the Lord. They taught me to do right and to always think right first. If you can talk right, you can do right, and if you do right, you're going to follow right. That was my role as a son, and I tried to teach Lem III those same principles, the way I was trained."

Lem is very clear about his duty as a dad. "A father's role is to train his kids," he says. "I thought Mom and Dad did an exceptional job. And in taking the path I took, I hoped to instill in Lem III those same principles. In his walk down future paths, my son will be guided by reverence and respect for the Lord."

The bond between father and son is evident. "We are friends and we share everything," Lemuel Barney III says. "Dad is just a real cool guy who I can talk to about anything. He has always been there for me and my sister."

These days, Lem's daughter Latrece Barney is a singer in New York City. "As a father, my dad was the best," she says. "He's always encouraged me to follow my dreams and is a very good man. Even though my mother and dad's marriage didn't turn out as we would've liked, my mother still believes that my dad was the best man she ever knew."

For Lem, it all comes down to friendship. "To have friends, you must be a friend," he says. And being Lem Barney's friend isn't about being an opportunist. Jim Thrower understands what Lem the friend is all about. "As a friend, he'll always give you a prayer and anytime you need him, he would always be there," Thrower says.

Lifelong friend Jerry Berry remembers Lem's transformation. "We were neighbors in 1968," he says. "Lem lived upstairs and I lived downstairs at the Regency Square. Mel Farr and even Stevie Wonder lived there. Marvin Gaye also frequented the building, visiting friends."

Berry says it's quite a remarkable metamorphosis between what Lem was then and what he is today. "Today, he doesn't just walk or talk the Christian ethic; he lives it day by day. I was never able to say, 'I love you' to a man till I met Lem. Because of Lem, I can tell my sons that I love them."

Berry feels that it's Lem's honesty and giving nature that taught him that important lesson. "Lem's the type of guy who would give you the shirt off his back. I've never met a more giving person. He was always a spiritual guy. Back then, he was always blessing his food and praying before bed. That road has led him to perhaps the role that best suits Lem Barney—the role of preacher."

"As a man of the cloth," Lem says, "I have to be honorable and respectful to the Lord first and then to myself. My role is to show others through example about the goodness and the greatness in life. Success only comes by giving testimony and showing that the Lord can pick them up from whatever despair they have, whatever problems, guilt, and shame."

Lem's role as a football player was to play his best while always being humble and to let others know the talent and skills he had were given to him by the Creator. "I am one with the Creator," he says. "I am to be humble in my walk because of the honor that has been bestowed upon me."

Lem thinks that people should lead by example—first in deed and then in word. "I try to encourage others to do the very best with the talents they've been given. Some people may want to denigrate themselves because they're not as tall or as fast as someone else. But people need to recognize they're unique. Everyone is given gifts, skills, and talents by the Lord to utilize and bring Glory to His name."

A man with similar athletic talents, Ronnie Lott thinks everyone would do well to comprehend Lem's message. "I look at myself as working to fulfill my destiny, like Lem is fulfilling his," Lott says. "Not just making great plays on the football field, but making great plays in life. I think the spiritual leadership he provides today makes great plays and a great difference in the lives of so many people. How do you want to leave the game of life? In Lem's ministering, he's doing God's good deeds, and I think that's something that all people should strive to do."

Family Man, Family Tree

"His father's name was Lemuel. His son's name is Lemuel. His son's son name is Lemuel. His name is Lemuel."

—The Barney Family Tree

THE IMPORTANCE OF FAMILY LIFE IS ingrained in Lem. With his warm, family-oriented upbringing, there was no doubt in his heart that he, too, would someday seek those things that his mom and dad found in each other—a love of God, a love for each other, and of course, a love of family.

"They gave us everything," Lem says. "Everything they had, they gave to me and my sisters. They always stressed the importance of family." Creating a family of his own was always a goal for Lem. To him, a family was something to hope for, work toward, and foremost, something to pray for.

"That's what life is all about," he says. Like most proud parents, he could talk endlessly about his two greatest accomplishments—his children. "Lem III is the oldest," Lem says. "He'll be 37 his year. He was born July 12, 1969—the day after man first walked on the moon." Lem feels that his birth was a miracle, just as every birth is a miracle. "To see the beginning of a life you helped create is truly humbling," he says.

Lem credits his dad—the original Lem Barney—for giving him the blueprint on how to build a healthy father-son relationship. "My dad was a profound guy without speaking more than a few words," Lem says. "When he did speak, it was always a conversation filled with the values of virtue. And like my conversations with my father, my son Lem and I will often share things in the Word and in the book." Lem III's spirituality makes his father proud because he's walking the right road and living up to his name. "The meaning of Lem in the Hebrew text is 'devoted or dedicated to God.'"

Lem lights up like a Christmas tree when he speaks of his daughter Latrece. "She was born February 27, 1974," he says. "She is such a joy. She's so very special and has made our lives even greater. She sings, writes, and arranges music. Professionally, she's even collaborated with Quincy Jones." Latrece has toured in London, Copenhagen, and Amsterdam and has received critical reviews for her work with Donna Summer. "She also sang the national anthem for the Pistons during the Bad Boys years."

His children are a tremendous source of pride, but Lem recalls a family loss where his faith once again helped him through a difficult time. "We had a stillborn birth between Lem and Latrece," he says. "Baby Barney was put in the grave. The Lord giveth and the Lord taketh away, blessed be the Lord."

Lem's faith and his family have kept him grounded as to what's important in life. "If I had to choose between two wonderful children and being in the Hall of Fame, I would pick the children," he says. "I would rather throw away my Hall of Fame enshrinement than to not have been able to raise these two wonderful children."

When Lem III followed in his father's football footsteps, Lem was there to listen and lend his advice. "I didn't want him to have the pressures of playing football like I did," Lem says. "I wanted to get him involved with tennis and golf as well. I advise parents not to force their kids to live out their own dreams, but Lem III wanted to play football." So Number 20 instructed his son in the fundamentals and mechanics of the game and stood back and hoped that he could become a solid player at Jackson State University.

"I also gave him a challenge," Lem says. "He had to maintain a minimum scholastic grade-point average in order to compete. I'm proud to say that he graduated from Jackson State and has a job that he enjoys as an elementary school teacher in the Houston public schools."

Lem III remembers what it was like growing up as the son of Lem Barney. "Back then, athletes lived in regular neighborhoods with regular people," he says. "We lived right next to the working-class people. It was a comfortable lifestyle, but with no Rolls Royce."

Lem III and his father still do a lot of things together. In his younger years, he and Lem were quite competitive. "We would play a lot of racquetball, and he would also take me to his football training camps," says Lem III. "I was a pretty good athlete and also played at Jackson State on a scholarship. But when it got to the point of either chasing the NFL dream or getting my education, I chose education. The bottom line is that there really could never be another football player like my dad."

Rather than pursue football, Lem III earned a degree in psychology. Today, he and his dad hang out and play golf and just get together for dinner or lunch. "We don't really have to do anything in order to enjoy each other's company," says Lem III. "One of the main things he's taught me is that whatever you set out to do, do it to the best of your ability and always take pride in your work—no matter what your occupation."

Lem III has seen all of his father's ups and downs, and Lem always comes through all right. "He keeps God first," says Lem III. "My grandmother always used to tell me, 'Give me my flowers now so I can smell them now, and don't wait till I'm in the grave to bring them to me.' I always make a concerted effort to tell Dad how I feel about him. My dad taught me faith, and that's the greatest legacy that he's given me. No matter how dark things get, he always tells me that you always need to have that faith." Lem III says he's working to instill in his son, Lemuel IV, the same principles that old Number 20 taught to him. "I'm proud to have my son named after such a good and great man," he says. And rightly so.

Life was exciting growing up the son of Lem Barney. Lem III's godfathers were none other than Mel Farr and Marvin Gaye. And he realized early in life just how successful his godfathers were. "My dad says, 'You know son, it doesn't matter how much money someone earns, he can never be as rich in spirit as I am.' Dad always kept the important things in life in perspective."

Latrece Barney also sees her father as a dedicated family man, remembering quite a normal upbringing with no great pomp and circumstance. "Being his daughter was like being anybody else's daughter," she says. "I know him as Dad, regardless of his celebrity status. It wasn't until I was grown that I started to realize how admired he was. Dad didn't seem at all like he was special. He was just warm, welcoming, and loving. Our family life was not very different from others."

Still, not everyone had Marvin Gaye, Smokey Robinson, Dave Bing, and Berry Gordy stopping by for house parties. "I do remember having the parties and having celebrities around," Latrece says. "It was very regular for me. My parents' anniversary was on Christmas Eve, and as usual, everyone was invited. For me and the family, it was the very best time of the year."

Like her father, Latrece leans on her faith to guide her life. "My Christian faith kept me balanced," she says. "At the parties, we would sing and dance, with Dad always being the life of the party. To this day, when the joy of the moment moves him, he'll get up on a table and start singing. When he's around, everyone's in awe of his energy and honesty. He commands attention without trying to. Mom's like that, too."

Latrece recalls the pain of her parents' separation. "As kids, we wondered if they really knew what they were doing," she says. "It was difficult, but we just needed to get to a point where we understood they needed to be happy. And as long as they stay friends, it'll be all right."

"Ultimately, it makes me happy to know that they're still young, they're happy and living their lives to the fullest. Dad is very happy with Jacci, and after all, their happiness is the most important consideration. Whatever they need to do to be happy, I will embrace."

Latrece has learned a lot from both parents. "From Dad, I've learned to put God first and everything will follow from there. From my mom, I've learned to follow your heart and be true to yourself."

"The greatest gift my dad gave me was my faith in God," she says. "My dad's legacy is being the light of the life of everyone he comes across. Dad is an extraordinary man, and everyone who he meets feels the same way about him."

She fondly remembers the good times growing up and traveling as a family. "We would go on a lot of vacations together," Latrece says. "I remember going to Las Vegas, Hawaii, Palm Springs, and other great spots."

"One of our favorite places to travel was to the drive-in movies. My parents loved to take us to the drive-in theater. They would get us ready for bed, pack the goodies, get in the car, and away we went. We would always fall asleep in the car while they watched the movie and put us to bed when we got home."

Spiritual and Motown music attracted Latrece to a singing career. "Growing up in Detroit, I related to life as a musician," she says. "Attending church was just a huge part of my life, and my involvement there kind of snowballed." When she was young, her mother recognized her talent for singing. Today, Latrece likens her style to Marvin Gaye and Gladys Knight and says she's enjoyed working with Quincy Jones, who she calls a remarkable entertainer and extraordinary musician.

While she lives in New York, she's still a Detroiter at heart and follows the team that her dad played for when she was a baby. "I'm a huge Lions fan," she says, "but I barely remember seeing Dad play. But when I get a chance to see film footage of his skills, I understand why so many people thought he was such an outstanding athlete."

Just thinking about her dad makes Latrece smile from ear to ear. "And when I start talking about him, I just can't quit," she says. "When I'm with my dad, I still look at him with awe. He's electrifying, he's the life of the party, and he's the celebration. It's been that way for as long as I can remember." Today, Latrece is happily single, but should she find Mr. Right, she says her dad is going to be one tough act to follow.

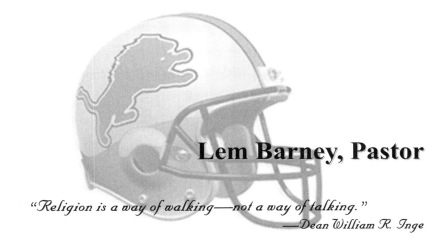

Lem Barney, Pastor

"Religion is a way of walking—not a way of talking."
—*Dean William R. Inge*

SPIRITUALLY, THE TABLE WAS SET AT home for Lem. God-fearing parents and a yearning for the Word set him on a spirited marathon in the direction of his ultimate goal line—the ministry. Slowly, steadfastly, and at an early age, Lem started his journey with the Lord. Talking with the Lord, walking with the Lord, walking the walk.

Today, as associate pastor at Detroit's Springhill Missionary Baptist Church, Lem believes in discipline and routine. "On Wednesday, I have songs of meditation and prayer and my own Bible study classes," he says. "On Wednesday night, if you can't make it during the day, you can go to the 7-9 p.m. Bible study prayer. It's about as much as I can get in during the week with group study. We nurture one another's growth."

Just as he would be called on for two-a-day football practices, Lem is now called on for two-a-day Bible studies classes. But for Lem, it's a labor of love. "I start every day off praying, singing, and applying the Word," he says. "I want to be an example to everyone of those truths that I touch during the day."

Lem's trek into the ministry started around 1975 when he was installed on the Board of the Prisons Fellowship Ministry. His duties involved traveling across the country spreading the Word of the Lord to prisoners. "The real reason most inmates go back to prison following their release is, in part, because they haven't gotten the Word," Lem says. "PFM works to make sure that during confinement and upon release, they continue to be linked with some church body of believers where they can continue to grow spiritually."

Washington lawyer Charles Colson, who played a key role in some of the darkest days of Watergate, saw the light while he was imprisoned. "Chuck was a tremendous lawyer in the D.C. area," Lem says, "and he had influenced some great business people—great men of wealth. He had a transformation in prison and was born again."

"While Colson was in prison, he authored a book titled 'Born Again.' It became a bestseller. From there, he started the prison fellowship work statewide. From that beginning, prison fellowship burst out all over the world. It was a good example for inmates, and it gave them a chance to have fellowship and worship the Creator."

Lem took his message to a place that had no streets—only prison bars. "I was on the national board of directors with Charles Colson," he says. "I would go into prisons around Michigan and other states to share the Word and my testimony."

He was entering an entirely different world. Upon entering each prison, he would be thoroughly checked by security. "After awhile, they knew everything about every visitor," Lem says. "But prison visits can't be spontaneous. You can't decide on Thursday to go in on a Friday. You have to make the arrangements in advance in order to be cleared."

Once inside, Lem would be taken to the chapel hall, where the inmates had gathered. But due to prison rules, he could only have a specified period of time for fellowship and to make sure the Word is received. "In my experience, there was no misconception of why each prisoner was there," he says. As testimony to the value of this work, upon release from prison, many former inmates became a part of Prison Fellowship program.

So what causes this transformation from hardened criminal to soulful believer? Lem thinks he has the answer. "The spirit does the work," he says, citing recent headlines where the Holy Spirit has persuaded criminals to turn themselves in after watching Mel Gibson's movie "The Passion of the Christ."

"When a person takes initiative to rededicate their life," Lem says, it is then they have found it. The spirit within them will drive a person to understand that they've been away too long, so they come back and rededicate their life to the church."

Whether preaching in a park or in the confined space of a prison, Pastor Barney knows his job. "You have to be bold for the Lord," he says. "Just speak boldly and have no afterthoughts. At that time, my only thought is in the present." Lem shares the Word of the Lord and hopes that someone will hear it and turn over their life to Him. It's the same thing on Sunday. "I let the spirit speak boldly in me," he says. "That's so people don't see me, but instead they see Him."

Lem's spiritual journey brought him to Springhill Missionary Baptist Church in Detroit, where he was made a lay minister by the late Dr. James E. Moss. Moss was the pastor and father-in-law of current pastor, Pastor Arthur.

Lem speaks highly of the man who, for the last eight years, has led the congregation of 600 believers. "Pastor Arthur is a good man with a good understanding of the Word," Lem says. "A great teacher and a great preacher." Having grown up in the Detroit area, Arthur was co-pastor for eight years under Moss and recalls his father in law's relationship with Lem. "He was influential in Lem's life because he was of the same generation and style as Lem's mother—and the two had a great rapport," Arthur says.

"Lem lived in Detroit—within walking distance of the church at that time. And when his mother would visit, she'd always say they were going to church as a family."

"My mother and Pastor Moss bonded right away," Lem says. "He was from Alabama and she was from Mississippi. Dr. Moss grew up at the height of the Jim Crow movement and also had an understanding of the South. He had a high academic degree for his generation in both the North and the South."

Being an athlete was good training for Lem to move into the ministry. "One of the main connections to his being an athlete and pastor is the team player concept," Arthur says. "He's always willing to do what's good for everyone and not just himself. Even though Lem has performed and met tens of thousands of people through his football career, he's able to sit in the back of the church and feel just as good as when he's conducting the service. He supports the other brethren and can take a back seat. He knows how to make other people feel good about who they are."

Pastor Arthur, who grew up idolizing Lem and his exploits on the football field, feels that Lem will be remembered for much more than his playing career. "His legacy will be in the church," Arthur says. "And while Lem could have been a sprinter, a golfer, basketball player, or even a tennis player, he missed all of the big money and exposure that would have gone with it at a later date. But wherever he goes, he presents himself as Reverend Barney. He wears it as a badge of honor."

When Lem worked with the Fellowship of Christian Athletes, he called the plays for the huddles and formations in his connection with the students and athletes. And his charges were quite impressed when they learned their coach was a member of the NFL Hall of Fame.

And when Lem was going through tough times, it was Dr. Moss who helped him get up off the floor. "Lem will mention it in sermons and in one-on-one consultations," Arthur says. "He has a very strong faith in God. It's great to see that he's rebuilt his life, and it's even better now than it was in his heyday playing football."

Lem is attending seminary and could be a full-time pastor now. It's clear he has the heart, the inclination, and the training to go all the way. But he still has a common touch. "People will remember Lem Barney best as an everyman's man and an everyperson's person," Arthur says. "He is a great assessor of what you need, and he can just plug into you on that level. He'll best be remembered as just a simple people lover." Perhaps most importantly, he will be remembered as a man who talked and walked with the Lord.

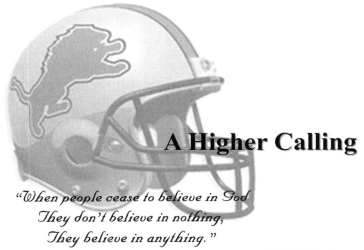

A Higher Calling

"When people cease to believe in God
They don't believe in nothing,
They believe in anything."

—*G. K. Chesterton*

$\mathcal{P}$ASTOR ARTHUR ASKED THE BIBLE students in his class a simple question. "If the Lord knocked on your door tonight, would you be ready to answer His call?" A man at the back of the class shouted out, "Yes!"

Arthur was not surprised to see who it was. It was Lem.

"When I first met him, I was starstruck because I had emulated him growing up on the playground," Arthur says. "But Lem didn't present himself as a star. He really acted just like a person. Lem is so approachable. He's so jovial and he makes you feel like you've known him your whole life."

As an associate pastor, Lem has the authority to carry out any of the functions of a pastor—from baptizing to communion to marriage to preaching, as required. He teaches Sunday School to about forty men and performs everything that a full-time pastor can. Lem's passion for performing his pastoral duties can be traced back to his childhood in church.

Today, he's still quite child-like in his love of the Word. "It was always a joyous time," Lem says. "We celebrated all of the Biblical holidays and all of the Biblical plays at church. I played everything from Jesus to a wise man. It was a great way to introduce people to the gospel. It was fun." And for the Easter egg hunt at Raleigh Methodist Church, Lem scavenged with the best of 'em.

"One thing about Jesus is that he did not preach denominationalism," Lem says. "You would be saved as long as you believe in Christ as the Lord and that He was the purpose. Sometimes, coming to church, people were not dressed as well as they might have been, while others dressed to the nines. While dressing well may have provided some folks with a sense of security while worshiping the Lord, He did not establish a dress code for worshipers. He just says, 'Come!'"

Lem's calling and the calling of all Christians manifests itself during Easter. "At Easter, I feel the joy and thrill and victory of discovering that He has risen," he says. "Go tell everyone that only His clothes are here. Hearing that on Easter Sunday morning creates a great feeling because it renews you and rejuvenates you." Easter never fails to give Lem an energetic feeling, and it strengthens his faith. It's a special time for him to witness the Lord's resurrection once again. "It's such a joy," Lem says. "He gave up His son for the entire world. *(John 3:16).* God so loved the world that He gave His only begotten son. I just thank God for that love and thank him for laying down his life for Lem Barney."

To those who do not have Jesus in their lives, Lem has some advice on fellowship. "You do it with gentleness and not harshness," he says. "The other person may have different views, but you can't argue, because the Word is not to be debated—it is to be agreed upon." As a teacher of the Word, Lem cites what Jesus taught. "He taught us what the Word is. And that is, He is the Word. He is the living Word. *(John 1:14)* And the Word became flesh."

To Lem, preaching isn't just preaching the Word on Sunday. He incorporates some interesting acronyms to make his point wherever and whenever he teaches. "It's a believer's responsibility to become educated in the Word," he says. "It simply means that we are to be the Word."

As one of his teaching tools, Lem uses the acronym HEART:

H—Hear the Word of God. *(Mark 4:23)* If anyone has ears to hear, let him hear, so you have to hear the Word.

E—Examine the Word—read and meditate on it. Search the scriptures everyday *(Timothy II 2:15)*. To do your best and to present yourself approved as one who does not need to be ashamed, but rightly divides the word of truth, so we have to go though this process.

A—Analyze the Word, read the Word.

R—Remember the Word. Remembering the Word comes from *Psalms 1:19 Verses 9-11*: How can a young man keep his ways dear? By living according to the Word of God.

T—Think the Word of God. We have to think about it and ponder it. *(Psalms 1:2-3)* Blessed is the man for his delights in the law of the Lord.

"So we have to hear the Word, examine the Word, analyze the Word, remember the Word, and think the Word," Lem says. "But the greatest thing about it is to apply the Word. We have to apply it in our everyday living."

Striving to become more educated in the Word, Lem feels a higher calling that has him seeking a master's degree in divinity for discipleship and Evangelism. "I was ready," he says. "It wasn't a difficult decision. I didn't say maybe. I lovingly said yes." He's now attending the Malone Theological School in Canton, Ohio, working on his degree in divinity. And he knows it will help him—and help others. "It's what I want to do for the rest of my life," he says.

Lem studies every day, and it's truly one of his passions. "Study increases my knowledge of God's Word. In it, I find the wisdom I need for life directly from God. The Word is nothing but the mind of God. The more I can get into His mind and study it, the better I will become in my own spiritual growth. It is a part of my spiritual fitness program."

One of Lem's greatest influences is former Secretary of Education Roderick Paige. "Dr. Paige was my head coach at Jackson

State," Lem says. "He's an intelligent man who set the mark high for his football players. He advised us to go to Vespers services on Sunday evenings." While Coach Paige never said it was mandatory, failure to attend would bring certain consequences. And Paige was always there to check the names off his list.

"If you didn't go," Lem says, "he would visit your room that night and ask for your meal tickets for the next two weeks. He believed that the spiritual side of life is just as important as the physical and the mental, and that we must have those three things together."

Paige remains as impressed as ever with his former player and lifelong friend. "It was immediately clear that Lem was special both as a person and as an athlete," he says. "What makes him so great is obviously his athletic ability. He was an All-American football player, and he was the kind of kid who could've been an All-American anything."

But Paige could see that Lem was raised right, too. "You notice the traits that his mother embedded in him—his professionalism and his gift for treating all people with respect. I'm proud of him as a person because he went through some strong difficulties, but I'm also proud of him for being a strong Hall of Fame athlete. I'm also proud that Lem found a calling."

Hall of Famer Deacon Jones feels the same. "Lem took a different path than I did," he says. "I'm very proud of him. He holds to his beliefs. Every day, he tries to strengthen himself as a human being. Most of all, he's not selfish and he looks out for others. That's the key, as far as I am concerned."

Jones and Lem go way back to the 1960s together. They've known each other for years, and Jones believes his old foe is following the right path in life. "Lem's best years are ahead of him," he says. "He's dealing with something now that's much bigger than himself. He's reaching out to change the world and make it a better place. That's an enormous task that God has given him, but Lem is up to the challenge."

Jones, too, thinks that Lem will be remembered for his quest to make a difference in the world. "This is much bigger than a football game," he says. "I hope to God that he has the strength and courage to work hard at it and make the sacrifice. I know he realizes how many people he can help now. Lem Barney will be remembered for what he does from here on out. It won't have anything to do with football. They'll all say that this great leader once played football. But he'll be remembered as a great giver in this world, too."

Lem credits his upbringing for preparing him for his higher calling. "I was a student and getting an education was intuitive," he says. "That drive was fostered by my mom, who really wanted me to become an educator." While he was in school, Lem was inspired by the classics of English literature. And he enjoyed studying his work assignments at home surrounded by his family. "I couldn't leave my books in my locker at night," he says. "Even when I wasn't assigned homework, I was driven to bring home new works, which took me to unexpected new adventures and knowledge."

Lem remembers why both his parents stressed a good education. His mother had only an eighth-grade education, and his father completed only the fourth grade. "For them, education was everything, and I learned to embrace that belief. I felt that the more education a person received, the larger the mind and future paychecks would become."

Lem initially went to college to realize his dream of becoming a professional football player. But while enrolled at Jackson State, his parents encouraged him to really apply himself in the classroom, too, so that he might have a career in education. "My mother used to say the difference between a teacher and an educator is that the teacher looks at paychecks, while the educator looks at minds," Lem says.

To make sure that he kept his focus, Lem's parents told him that if he didn't earn a high GPA, he wouldn't be allowed to play football. "Education is a foundation for life," he says. "You must have an education to successfully make it in our society. Because my parents never had the educational options I did, it was necessary for them to enter the workforce early in their lives to support and maintain a family with four kids. That's why they always stressed the value of an education.

† Lem Barney †

As Lem works toward his master's in theology, his parents must surely be proud. "This study will help me grow as a spiritual Christian and teach me about the sovereign word of God," he says. "Because of this, I'll be able to share the good news of the gospel and try to encourage young people to go into the faith as a study. I'd like to be that salt and that light for the young people in my daily life."

Lem, left, with good friends Linda
Hendricks, Ted Hendricks (right), and
friend at a Napa Valley golf event.

Greg Kelser, Lem, Thom Seafron,
and Jim Brandstatter at a Davenport fundraiser golf classic. They
finished in first place.

Pro Football Hall of Famer Leroy
Kelly, of the Cleveland Browns,
and guest join Lem at a Napa Valley
golf event.

Lem and former teammate Gail Cogdill
at the Pontiac Silverdome.

Horace King and Lem at Detroit's Ford
Field for Lions Alumni Day in 2003.

It's hard to find a happier couple than Lem and Jacci.

Lem's sister Varina with niece Tiffany.

Lem welcomes his old friend Bobby Mitchell with open arms.

Jennifer Hilliker of Immortal Investments Publishing and Lem take a break from working on The Supernatural to pose for a photo.

Lem and friends dress the part for Deacon Jones's Western-themed golf outing.

At the Silverdome with former teammates Mike Weger (left) and Gail Cogdill.

Two Pro Football Hall of Famers: Lem and "L.T."—the one and only Lawrence Taylor.

John and Sylvia Macky pose with Lem.

Marquette University's Marissa Thrower (left) and Elizabeth Ford join Lem at the Michigan Sports Hall of Fame banquet.

Jacci's family: Great-great aunt Jennie Thomas with great-great cousin Raymond Williams (top left); sister Dora Thomas and nephew Robert Ballard (top right); brother Leon Harper and family (bottom left) and former President Jimmy Carter with Dora.

Aunt Carrie, Valeria, Agnes, Marie, Tea, and Varina visiting family in San Bernardino, California.

Great niece Tyra and her family.

Lem's dear friends the Simpsons. From left to right, Pam, Donnie Jr., Donnie Sr., and Dawn.

Lem and Jacci celebrate Christmas with sisters-in-law Dora Thomas, Rose Harper-Elder, Mildred Harris, and brother-in-law Bob Ballard in Washington, D.C., in 2002.

The Barney's many loved nieces, great nieces, nephews, and great nephews.

"Mikie" (left) a dear friend to the Barneys, shares a laugh Lem and Jacci's sister Dora.

Jacci's brother Bob Ballard, Lem, and Sugar Ray Leonard's brother Roger Leonard.

Lem's sister Lemelda celebrates Christmas.

Lem and Jacci (right) with her sister Rose.

A family photo of Albert, Marie, La Joi, and Jenny

Proud papa Lem with his daughter, LaTrece, on her wedding day.

Lem's namesakes: His son, Lem Barney III, holds grandson Lem IV.

Three generations of Barneys: Lem (right), Lem III (center), and grandson Jamir.

Lem and Varina pose with Lem's Hall of Fame bust in 2000.

Lem with his sisters Lemelda (left) and Varina in their hometown of Gulfport, Mississippi.

Lem in his classic derby.

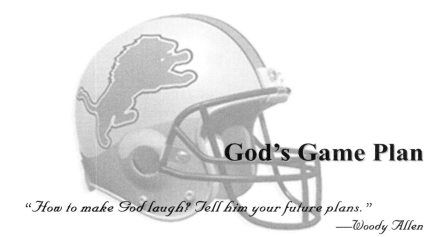

God's Game Plan

"How to make God laugh? Tell him your future plans."
—Woody Allen

ON A CHILLY SUNDAY MORNING ON Detroit's west side in early 2000, the snow was softly falling. A white man and his sister were on their way to church, but not to their traditional Sunday Greek Orthodox church service. Instead, in their search for some of that old-time religion, they were on the way to a humble, black Baptist church. They had one problem, however. They were lost.

Two white kids in search of a black church who didn't have a clue as to where the former football star and newly ordained minister named Lem Barney was going to preach. They had an invitation, but no map. As the brother searched his mind for guidance, his sister sat patiently, while he tried to figure out how to find the church that his friend, the Reverend Lem Barney, had invited them to visit. In their quest, they stopped at three churches in the vicinity to ask, "Is this where Lem Barney is speaking?" Three times, the young man came back to the car without directions, and each time, he felt a little more stupid as he entered the car.

The young man turned to his sister and said, "Now I know how black people feel when they need help in an all-white neighborhood.

Everyone I talked to was very nice, but somehow, I felt like an outsider who didn't belong."

It stopped snowing. The fallen snow began a transformation from white to black as it melted into the gray, wet streets on a gloomy Super Bowl Sunday morning in the Motor City.

"There's another Baptist church over there," the sister said. "It's the Spring Hill Missionary Baptist Church. Could that be it?"

It was.

In moments, they were inside. The pair was easy to spot in the otherwise all-black crowd. But a beautiful thing happened—no one noticed them as they nestled in next to their brothers and sisters. Their eyes darted around the wood-paneled, domed church. Music bounced around inside the modest surroundings and warmed the chill of a drafty structure that had seen better days. Still, that didn't matter. Inside, the preaching and singing of the gospels warmed the faithful. A respectful gentleman who wore a neat black suit with white gloves escorted the two visitors to their seats. Soon, these two believers fit in. They sang timidly at first, as the congregation sang at the top of their lungs.

Ain't that good news. If you call on Jesus ...
Ain't that good news if you call on Jesus!

Caught in the moment of soulful hand clapping and passionate displays toward the Lord, the two felt the rhythm of their black brothers and sisters.

"All you have to do is call on Jesus!"

The two newcomers sang at the top of their lungs, with all their heart. This old-time religion had indeed touched their souls. The sister smiled at her brother and he smiled back. In turn, they smiled at all their new brothers and sisters on this cold Sunday morning in January. But it was getting warmer by the second inside the church. Pastor Arthur stepped to the pulpit to preach. As he did, members of the congregation fanned themselves.

"Brothers and sisters, today is Super Bowl Sunday," he said. "And you know that every day is Super Bowl Sunday in the service of the Lord."

"You got that right," said a heavyset woman in a yellow hat.

"All you have to do is call on Jesus!" said the preacher.

"Amen! Call on Jesus—you got that right!" came a shout from the congregation.

"All you have to do is call on Jesus, brothers and sisters. How many times do we forget that? How many times do we keep the Lord out of our game plan? Well today, on Super Bowl Sunday, I just want to remind you to call on Jesus today, tomorrow, on Super Bowl Sunday, and every day in between."

"Call on Jesus!" the pastor shouted.

"Amen, brother!

"Call on Jesus!"

"Hallelujah!

The white brother and sister looked at each other and smiled.

Pastor Arthur continued. "It may be cold outside, but inside it's delightful. The Lord is good. God is good. Let us pray. Lord, thank you so much for being so good to us. Thank you for giving us the spirit of worship. We're glad to be in your service, shouldering up the cross. Thank you for being that good news. Yes, all you have to do is call on Jesus.

You are so good. I ask in the name of Jesus. Amen."

"Amazing Grace" echoed from every corner of the church. In moments, the sweet, soulful sounds of the congregation united in prayer and music to produce a perfectly tuned voice of one.

"Today, we have the privilege of having with us, the newly ordained minister Lemuel Barney. Lem's a man who has been gifted athletically, now we hope and pray that God will bless him prophetically as he works toward a new level of preaching in the service of the Lord. Brothers and sisters … Reverend Barney."

Lemuel Barney grabbed the spotlight and the pulpit, as a church full of faithful football fans and fans of the gospel waited for the Hall of Famer to shine his light on the Word.

"Amazing Grace!" he said. "I was blind, now I see. … I was blind, now I see. Brothers and sisters, you can't get singing like that at home," Lem said as he flashed his trademark smile. The church was getting warmer.

"God is good. And [Pastor Arthur] is so good. I love him. His father-in-law was the great Pastor Dr. James Moss. He was the greatest man that I ever knew, and the Pastor follows in his footsteps.

"Today, I want to talk about God's game plan," said Reverend Barney. "I just got in today from Atlanta, where they're preparing for Super Bowl XXXIV. I was honored to be there to celebrate as they renamed the Humanitarian Award after 'Sweetness,' the late, great Jacksonian Walter Payton.

"I thank God that I was able to get here today, I didn't know if I was going to be able to. This morning, 400,000 good people of Atlanta were still without power due to the weather. Still it's in God's game plan that I got here today. I learned that as brothers and sisters, we must not take anything for granted. We must be on the same page with the Maker. Because God has a plan, and we're all part of God's game plan.

"God is good. God is so good. Let's read from his playbook— God's game plan. Let's turn our attention to John, Chapter Four, and talk of the Samaritan woman and where she met up with the Lord at Jacob's well.

"Amen, brother!"

"Amen, Reverend Barney!"

"You got that right!"

The shouts came from the congregation. Not surprisingly, two of the shouts came from the white brother and sister who arrived late for the service. They all gathered as part of God's game plan.

"I want to talk about a Samaritan woman," Reverend Barney said. "Now the Samaritans were half Jew and half gentile. They were outcast by the Jews. Well, this woman met Jesus near Jacob's well and he said to her, 'Woman, give me to drink.'

"She asked him, how did he—a Jew—ask this woman for a drink of water? Jesus needed to go through Samaria because God made a plan for this woman. For it was God's game plan for this sinful woman to meet Jesus and find in him the living water. Brothers and sisters, there are different stages in which we come to believe, and many ways in which the Lord opens our eyes to his plan.

"Urgency. Jesus moved with urgency. Moving with urgency is what Jesus was all about. You cannot go back to yesterday or last year. You have to be impressed with Jesus. He knew his time had not come, but he knew his hour was coming. He walked in the confidence of his father's timetable. Yet, even though he knew he would be offered up as a living sacrifice for the world, he lived every day as if it would be his last. Urgency and obedience stay with me now.

"I cannot imagine Jesus ever being late for anything. He was always there on time. He may not come when we want him, but he's always on time. That is part of God's game plan. God, too, has a game plan for our lives.

"Jesus was on time to meet the Samaritan woman. In fact, he was already waiting for her to arrive, already anticipating what he was going to say to her. And he knew exactly what she needed.

"Jesus opens our eyes to our own needs."

Raising his voice now, Reverend Barney stressed his point. "He was there to open her eyes to her own needs," he says. "He was there to tell her that she did not need physical water; the water she needed was living water that was breathed with the spirit to satisfy a living soul!"

"Amen!"

"Yes!"

"You got that right!"

The shouts came from young and old, from black and white.

"So often, we try to quench our thirsty nature with things of the world. Unless we have living water, we will suffer from spiritual dehydration. We need the living water. Are you ready for the living water?…Brothers and sisters, are you ready for the living water? Come see the man! He knows all your struggles. He knows what you need. He has been there through 42 generations. The prophets foretold his coming.

"Through his birth, his crucifixion, his resurrection. Come see the man! He knows what you need. He has you in his game plan. Are you ready for drink from his living water? Come see Jesus and drink from the living water!"

The Reverend Barney sat down as the choir started to sing and the organ started to play the heavenly hymns, the newly ordained minister bowed his head in prayer. In moments, the congregation would begin filing out of the warm church and out into the cold streets of Detroit. Outside, the snow was beginning to melt and turn into water that ran slowly down the street. Some of this freshly melted snow found its way to the city's sewer system, releasing its essence into the draining wells.

Some in the congregation exited the church in a hurry and headed home to dinner with family and friends and perhaps to watch a little football on this Super Bowl Sunday. And some stayed a little longer, huddling together to share parting words and the Word. In moments, they, too, would be going home, perhaps filled with the living water of Jesus and a better understanding of God's game plan.

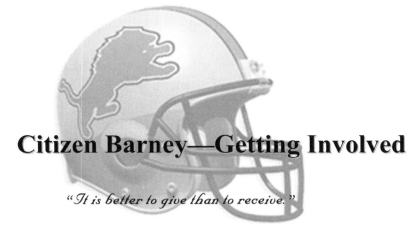

Citizen Barney—Getting Involved

"It is better to give than to receive."

*I*N A WORD, LEM IS A MAN INVOLVED IN his community. And the word on the street is that his word is gold. If a school needs a keynote speaker, call Lem. If a church needs a sermon, call Lem. If some prisoners need some guidance, call Lem.

Involved, visible, talking the talk, and walking the walk.

Whenever Detroit Lions community affairs director Tim Pendell needs someone to go out into the community on a goodwill mission, Lem is often the first person he calls. "Lem is just a very charismatic, good person, who does a lot for many people," Pendell says. "He is a giving person who we're proud to send out to various charity and community events."

Lem enjoys working with Pendell, combining his old team with his community work. "He's dubbed me the ambassador for the Lions, and I go out and speak to different organizations," Lem says. "Tim has a lot on the ball and keeps things going in the community."

Pendell, who's known Lem for 20 years, is thankful for Lem's continuing contributions to the team. "As great as he was as a player, he is an even better person, and it's evident in his responses to us. Lem Barney always shows up and represents himself and the Detroit Lions in the best way possible."

Being out in the public is something that comes naturally to Lem. "I love communicating with people, I love to touch people, and it's a joy and an honor to be asked to be a keynoter," he says.

Lem has clarity where charity is needed. It's a part of who he is and part of his upbringing. Old Number 20 always gave something back to the game, to the community, to his family of brothers and sisters. His spirit of sharing and helping has flowed from the gulfstream waters of Mississippi to the streets of the Motor City.

Joe Hoskins, Lem's team captain at Jackson State, won several championships as a high school football coach in Detroit. He found he could always count on his old friend. "Lem is second to none, because he's been such a dear friend," Hoskins says. "He has an unwavering commitment. Whenever I called him up to speak to my kids, he was always there."

This is one citizen who is always charitable with his heart, mind, and time. If there was a brother in prison, he went. A sister who had lost her way, he was there, making a beeline to intercept her pain in the same way he would intercept a football during his playing days. Well, those were his playing days. Today they're his praying days. Often, you'll find him at a benefit, a church function, or a charity event, more than likely giving the invocation to start the proceedings, and then later lending his words and talents as a way to pay off his debt to his fellow brothers and sisters.

Benny White remembers the impact Lem had on his life. "I was a senior in high school and I was playing in the annual high school all-star game in Detroit," he says. "I attended Northern High School. Lem was one of the celebrity coaches. Dave Bing coached the other team. Since I was a basketball player, I wanted to play for Dave's team. I had met Dave at his basketball camp a couple of years before and wanted to play for him, but they put me on Lem's team."

That's when their friendship began, and it has only grown since. "As a coach, Lem is enthusiastic. He stresses the fundamentals—to play together and to have some fun. The first day I was there, Lem gave me a ride home. I was a little guy at the time, only 5-foot-8, but Lem always seemed to believe in the little guys. I ended up becoming the most valuable player in that particular game." After meeting

Lem's wife, Benny felt like a part of their family. "When I graduated from college, we continued the relationship, and it's grown from there. One of Lem's habits is to give people he likes nicknames. My Lem name was One. 'Cuz you're one in a million,' Lem told me."

Lem became much more than a football player to Benny. He became a father figure. "Since that time, he introduces me as his younger brother," Benny says. "People really think that I'm his biological brother because of our close relationship."

When Lem believes in something or someone, it's all or nothing. And Lem believes in giving of himself. When he had a chance to travel with fellow NFL pros Tom Dempsey, Bob Lilly, Ernie Wright, and Tom Matte to Asia in 1971 as part of a USO tour, he took his unique outlook and philosophy with him. The purpose of the trip was to visit wounded troops in the Philippines, Tokyo, and Guam and was sponsored by the U.S. Department of Education. "We spent three hours a day visiting the soldiers who had suffered the pains of Vietnam," Lem says. "We would try to cheer them up and thank them for being committed to serving and protecting the country. We would sign autographs and pass out decals. Our mission was to inspire them, but in truth, I received far more inspiration from them because of their courage."

Lem pauses to regain his composure. "Some had arms and legs blown off and were terribly injured," he says. "And it was those brave, injured soldiers who complimented us for our inspiration. But we were the people inspired. I'll never forget that trip and how courageous these men were."

Years later after Lem had retired from the NFL and was working with the gas company, he and a friend were having breakfast one morning when a young fellow walked up to their table and introduced himself. "You're Lem Barney, aren't you?" he said. "I just wanted to thank you again for visiting me and lifting my spirits when I was in the Pacific. You probably don't remember me, but you came to my bed and we had a short conversation. I appreciated your gesture that day. In the military, I was awarded two berets for my service in the Pacific and would like very much for you to accept one of them. I've given the other beret to my son."

Lem was truly touched by the man's gesture and was moved to tears. Lem's mind was on that soldier, the war he had gone though, and also on those men and women still engaged around the world in the fight to protect our way of life. But he's conflicted by the foolishness of men who would wage such carnage. Lem believes that love can find a way to win the day.

"Our Master said there would always be war because there is not enough love in the world," Lem says. "Christ told us to 'love one another as I have loved you. You must love one another, and if you do this, then all of the world will know that you are my disciples.' With this philosophy as my weapon, I still believe that love will triumph over war."

Lem deeply believes that all people are brothers and sisters of the Lord and that we were created in His image in order to bring us together in peace. "I believe that the hug will win more wars that any sword," Lem says. "Those who live by the sword must die by the sword, and those who live with love will live on with love eternally."

Then he offers his plea:

"Dear children, let us not love with tongue and in word, but let us love with deed and in truth."

Whether in a Mississippi church or a Motown ghetto, if it's a good cause that brings people together in a united way, Lem will be there. To borrow a phrase from Marvin Gaye, if you need Lem, just call him. Cuz there ain't no mountain high enough to keep Lem from getting to you.

A Heal of a Time

*"Do you hear the children weeping, o my brothers?
Ere the sorrow comes with years?"*
—*Elizabeth Barrett Browning*

"CHILDREN ARE OUR GREATEST asset," Lem says. "Contained within them is all the goodness of God. They are the flowers of the earth. It's up to all of us to help them grow up strong and pure."

Lem was on his way to Buell Elementary School in Flint, Michigan, to help provide some kind words and healing help after Kayla Rolland, a beautiful 6-year-old child, was tragically shot to death by a fellow first-grader in February of 2000. The incident was yet another horrific reminder of how violent our world is. It was a gaping wound inflicted on the hearts of America.

On another dark day in April of 1999, at Colorado's Columbine High School, two students shot thirteen people to death before taking their own lives. This was yet another sad picture of the world we live in. And how, in the blink of an eye, it could all come crashing down on anyone. The lesson we learned was that even our children aren't always safe. That was the point behind today's lesson plan, for people in the suburbs and in deprived ghettos. It was gnawing at Lem as he made his trip to Flint.

"Children not safe from other children," he said. Lem shook his head as he looked out the car window. How bad had things become when a 6-year-old girl's life could be taken away in school at the hands of a classmate? It was unfathomable, but the horrible truth in today's society is that kids are killing kids. It was not a nightmare, it was reality, and it was what compelled Lem to go to the site of the tragedy. He had to be there to try to ease the pain of a school full of elementary students mourning the death of one of their own playmates.

A violent world weighed heavily on Lem. In the car, the rain came down in buckets as the words poured out. "There's just no place for violence in society, and there's definitely no place for it when it comes to kids," he said, as tears began to well up in his eyes. He looked over at nine-year-old Allie Gasiorowski, the daughter of a close friend, who was accompanying him on his good will trip to Flint.

"Hey Allie, what are you going to do for the kids?" he asked.

"I'm going to read them a couple things I wrote," she said, as she paused to look outside. "I hope it makes them feel better."

"I'm sure it will, Allie. I'm sure it will," he said as he patted her head and looked out at the gray Michigan skies. "Just to know that you care will make them all feel a little better."

After an hour-and-a-half ride through hard rains, the healing team, composed of a little girl and a Hall of Fame preacher, arrived at the Buell School. And when they did, the rain began to let up. The unlikely duo walked side-by-side up to the school.

"Allie, are you excited?" Lem asked.

"Yes. Let's go do some good," she said in her squeaky voice.

As they entered the gymnasium, little Allie had one last question. "Hey, Lem," she said, "do people ever confuse you with Barney the purple dinosaur?"

Lem just smiled and looked at his little helper. Allie already had her game face on. She smiled back at Lem. And now they were ready to do some good for the good children of Buell Elementary School. Allie was up first. She eased into a poem about herself called "Let Me Introduce Myself," which ended like this:

I like to draw.
I like to do art.
And use the talents that are deep in my heart.
So if you get sad, like sometimes we all do.
Just think of all the cool things that you know how to do.

The healing process had begun. The children applauded the young poet. She grinned back at them with a humble, caring smile, then turned the microphone over to Lem.

"That was great, wasn't it?" he asked the group. "Allie is a real hero. Do any of you know what a hero is?"

The arms shot up with answers.

"It's about being good."

"It's about doing good things."

"Yes, yes, exactly," Lem said. "It's both about doing good things and being good. And you know what?"

"What?!" they shouted back.

"People doing good things come in all shapes, sizes, and ages," he said.

Enthusiastic smiles greeted Barney, the type of response usually reserved for purple dinosaurs of the same name.

"All our lives, from the moment we're born, we're all heroes," Lem continued. "We are all blessings from God. And from the moment you first try to speak, we're nothing more than a recorder playing back the lessons we have learned. Do you know what a recorder is?"

"Yes—a VCR!" shouted a child sporting a Denver Broncos jersey.

"Exactly," answered Lem. "Your life is like a VCR. You can learn something and then play it back. From the time you're born, you begin your life as a recorder. It's like that Energizer battery bunny—it goes on and on, keeps going and going. So what you want to do is record good things in your life so that when you play them back, you'll get what? That's right. The same things, good things that you recorded and can play back over and over."

The children smiled.

"Now we all know about the incident that happened here," Lem said. "The whole world knows about that incident. We're glad that you let us come here today, to share in the healing process. And what we want to say, what the entire world wants to say to you, is, 'Hey, kids, we love you."

"We love you!" they cried back. The children looked on, smiling slightly as their teachers nodded in approval.

"And we want you to become the beautiful blossomed flowers that the Lord wanted you to become," Lem said. "Right now, you're tiny seeds, but the Lord has intended for you to become great giant flowers. Beautiful blossomed flowers with fragrance for the ladies. Robust and strong flowers for the gentlemen."

Lem paused as he looked over the young students sitting with legs crossed, staring up at him from the gymnasium floor.

"Who would like to become a giant tree?" he asked. "Who would like to grow up to become a great oak tree?"

Many of the children raised their hands. Just as many raised their voices.

"I do, I do," they shouted individually. "I do!" they shouted in one voice.

"Well, right now," Lem said, "your seeds are being nurtured by your teachers and your parents, so your seeds can grow and you can become anything that you want to be."

Lem paused for a question.

"How many of you know what you would like to be?" he asked. The kids shouted back with their answers, but more importantly, they shouted back with their dreams.

"A teacher!"

"Good," Lem said. "We need more teachers."

"A preacher!"

"Good, the world needs more preachers," he said.

"A fireman!"

"Good, we need firemen to put the fires out," Lem said.

"A cop!"

"Good, we need more police officers."

"A basketball player!"

"Good, work on your skills and stay in school."

"A doctor!"

"Good, we need more doctors," Lem said.

"A nurse!"

"Good, a lot of sick people need a good nurse," Lem said.

Lem stopped, pausing to look down at doctors, nurses, teachers, preachers, and firemen. "Right now is the best time to find out what you want to become," he said. "It was not too long ago that I was sitting right where you are. I was eight years old, and I wanted to become a professional football player.

"Do you know what people told me? They said I would get hurt, smashed to smithereens. They told me that I could never make it—that I could never do it."

Lem paused again, connecting with their wide-eyed gazes.

"But whenever someone told me I couldn't do it," he said, "I would try even harder. I kept trying. I had a great mother and father who supported me in all the things that I wanted to do. And later, after I had worked very hard, I had the opportunity to play Little League football, and I continued to grow.

"From grade school to high school, I continued to play football. Eventually, I earned a scholarship to play football in college. And that really helped my mom and dad out. Going to college is very expensive, and a scholarship made it possible.

"It's going to cost a lot to live your dreams," he said. "It would be nice to help your moms and dads by earning a scholarship."

"Yeah!" the kids shouted.

"Well, you can do it!" Lem told them. "Work on your skills and your talent. And if you do that, you can win scholarships.

"Now when I went to school and got drafted some 34 years ago, how many of you were around?" Lem said, laughing. "Not many. I guess I'm an old dinosaur. Let me ask you something. If you were going to be a dinosaur, what kind would you be?"

The children shouted out various answers and then one child shouted out, "A Tyrannosaurus Rex."

"A T-Rex," Lem said and smiled. "A T-Rex—the giant of all dinosaurs. That's the kind of dinosaur I would be.

"Be the best!" he said. "Be the best that you can be.

"So after I was drafted by the Detroit Lions, I was very excited. Why was I so excited? Because I realized a dream come true. And all those people who had told me that I couldn't do it were wrong. They told me that I would get beat up, they told me that I would get torn from limb to limb. Well, I made it, and my dream came true.

"And you know what happened on the first play when the ball was thrown my way? Well, let me tell you, I intercepted the ball thrown by a great quarterback and ran it all the way back for a touchdown. It was so much fun that I spiked the ball in the end zone and looked up and said, 'Lord, is this going to be easy.'

"It was very rewarding to realize a dream that I had from the time I was eight years old, about the age you kids are now. So right now, you can start the journey. You can become anything that is in your heart."

"A teacher."

"You can do it!"

"A doctor."

"You can do it!"

"A football player!"

"You can do it."

Lem reminded the children that God has given them all different talents and gifts.

"Now you may know that I'm ordained minister," he said. "How many of you pray?"

With that, many hands went up.

"Pray all the time," Lem advised the children. "If you have to sneak away to the bathroom and pray, pray there. Before a test, say a little prayer ... kind of like that song from the Sixties—that Dionne Warwick song..."*The moment I wake up, when I comb my hair and put on my makeup ..."*

The children laughed.

Lem smiled at them.

"You know what I mean," he said. "I say a little prayer for you. The only way to communicate with the Almighty is through prayer.

"Now, I want to finish with this little story about a farmer who was trying to harvest his wheat. He was having a little problem separating the wheat from the weeds, because they grow together.

"To make a long story short, what he had to do was let the wheat and weeds grow together until harvest time. Then, he would gather the weeds and burn them and harvest the wheat and bring it to the barn—the Barney."

Lem laughed at his little joke. "You see the moral of the story is burn up the bad things in your life and keep the good things," he said. "Remember your life is like a recorder.

"Now," he said, "let me tell you that story in a rap version. And here's what I want you kids to do. Allie show them. When I say Grow Seeds! Grow Seeds! Grow Seeds! Grow! You go to the left waving your arms, then the right, then wave to the ground and then to the sky. Got it?

"Good!"

With that, Lem started making all the appropriate rap noises as he sang verse after verse in this his wheat-and-weed rap.

"A farmer went to the field to sow
He gathered his seeds, watered them, and watched them grow
Grow seeds, grow seeds, grow seeds, grow!"

The children waved their arms frantically as they rapped.

"Now the moral of this Gospel rap
Is that Satan has an awful trap
He's divided the church and made God sad
Instead our Lord says leave it all be . . .
'I will judge you all for eternity'
That is when your right time will come
And you will grow on and grow strong
Grow seeds, grow seeds, grow seeds, grow!"

"The moral," Lem said, "is great seeds produce great crops. And all of you right now are in your purest form. May all of you grow up to become all that you want in life. We're going to keep a close eye on you. We're going to watch all your seeds grow. As you continue to go through life, grow through life and ultimately glow through life. God bless you all."

After Lem signed a few autographs and spoke with some of the thankful teachers, it was time for him and Allie to go. Outside, it had stopped raining. In the distance, the sun did all it could to break through the clouds. Spring was in the air. The earth was soaked with God's rain. All the ingredients were now in place. And somewhere on the grounds of this tiny school with a wounded heart, a flower started to grow upward toward the heavens.

Grow seeds. Grow seeds. Grow seeds. Grow!

EGO - EGO + HERO = TWO ZERO

$$(\mathcal{E}\text{-}\mathcal{E} + \mathcal{H} = 20)$$

N O, THIS ISN'T A NEW FORMULA developed by Einstein. It's not the theory of relativity either, but it is relevant. It's merely a formula of how to become a hero—a blueprint for how this Number 20 has always lived his life.

"Do you know what ego stands for?" Lem asked.

The respondent struggled for the answer, encouraged by the tireless preacher. "Come on, let me show you," Lem said. Pulling a pen from his jacket, he started scribbling on a napkin. "This is a play from God's playbook…Ego is:

E for Edging

G for God

O for Out

"When you have too much EGO, you're Edging God Out."

Another smile followed, the preacher was teaching now. It was on this praying field, not the playing field, that Lem felt the most at home. "When we Edge God Out, we get into trouble," he says. "It's like playing a game without penalties, referees, or rules," he says. "Everything and anything goes. It then becomes a story of a monster of the midway. A monster fiercer than Dick Butkus ever was—a monster called ego." He capped his pen tightly to emphasize his point.

The respondent looked on, almost hoping that the lesson from God's playbook would continue.

"Do you understand?" Lem asked with concern. The student nodded, but not convincingly enough to end the lesson.

"Here, let me show you," Lem said, uncapping the pen and picking up another piece of paper. Slowly, he began to illustrate how God can get to you and how Satan appeals to you. "This is something we studied in class the other day," Lem said. "There are ways that God speaks to you and there are ways that the devil tempts you. Once you know the right way, then you'll be able to protect yourself and focus on the right path to stay on."

According to Lem, one appeals to your heart, and the other appeals to your ego.

"It goes like this," he said, as he started to draw a circle with a cross in the middle of it.

"Ego—when a person is egotistical and wants everything his way, he is edging God out. We cannot always be selfish. We have to share, care, and give, or the ego can become the problem that edges God out."

Lem's formula for success is rather simple. He puts God first and everything else second. And he does one other thing. Lem divorces himself from his ego, and because he has, fame has followed him. That is how it works for this hero, who is a member of no less than seven halls of fame.

In 2004, Lem attended the fiftieth anniversary of the Michigan Sports Hall of Fame, of which he is a member. It was the largest class ever inducted, a group that included Mike Lucci, Chris Spielman, Pat LaFontaine, Joe DeLamielleure, Jim Abbott, Herb Deromedi, George Puscas, Fred Stabley Sr., Mike Ilitch, and Bill Davidson.

Lem thought back to 1985, when he was first inducted into the Michigan Sports Hall of Fame. Respectful of all the honors he has received over the years, Lem keeps his ego in check with a grounded perspective. "These are honors that I never thought about while I was playing," he says. "I was more concerned about my play. I just wanted to be on top of my game. The seven Pro Bowls were a great tribute during my playing days. To receive those honors is a reminder that what I did during those years was above and beyond the call of duty."

So which honor does Lem covet most? "My Mississippi Sports Hall of Fame means a great deal to me because it's from my home state," he says. "My Michigan Sports Hall of Fame is very special, too, because it's from my adopted home." He was also honored by the Blue-Gray Hall of Fame, the Southwest Athletic Conference, and the African-American Athletics Sports Hall of Fame. And of course, being inducted into the Pro Football Hall of Fame was a huge thrill. "They were all great honors," Lem says, "but the greatest of all awards is my membership in the Lord's Hall of Fame."

Lem understands he has not edged out God in his recognition of fame. And it shows in his gratitude when he accepts an honor or accolade. "Each of my speeches was from the heart and from feelings and memory," he says. "I don't like prepared texts. I like to speak right from the heart. It's a real joy for me to be in the public eye and to be around these great people. It's humbling to know that at the NFL Hall of Fame, you're one of only a few on that team of tremendous talent, with a group of great people and athletic heroes."

Lem knows that great players like him are often seen as role models. The great Gale Sayers knows better than most what that's like. But he doesn't necessarily buy into it. "When I look for heroes," he says, I don't really think of athletes. I look at regular people like my dad. When I was attending college, some people didn't think I could make it. My dad encouraged me with five words: 'Gale, you are good enough.' That's all I needed to hear—somebody who believed in me, and my dad did."

He says he never tried to be like anyone else. He only tried to make himself better. "I saw what Jim Brown was doing and I asked myself how I could make myself a better player," he says. Later, his brother encouraged him to get his master's degree. "I respected the great players, but my dad and my brother were my heroes."

Former Steelers great Mel Blount believes a hero is someone who perseveres through the tough times and sets an example for dealing with life's difficult journeys. "A hero is someone who has a tremendous amount of influence on others and who exemplifies life," he says. "Lem has seen the rain, he's seen the sunshine, he's seen the storms, but what he's been able to do is maintain who Lem Barney is. A lot of people fall on hard times and they either end up homeless or dead. But this guy has been able to take those experiences and use them to shape his character into who he is today. To me he is a hero. He is a hero because of where he came from and what he is on the inside. Lem has seen the good, the bad, and the ugly. He has been able to maintain his dignity and his sense of self-worth."

As a child, Heisman Trophy winner and NFL Hall of Fame running back Marcus Allen was intrigued whenever he watched Lem play. "Lem was one of my heroes and one of the first players I looked up to," Allen says. "He was a very charismatic player with a unique style that attracted me to him very early. My first position in football was cornerback. I loved to hit people and make interceptions like the great players did. Most young kids looked to the offensive players to idolize, but Lem stood out, even though he was on defense. On the field, he became the person most people wanted to watch." Years after hanging up his cleats, it is Lem's exploits off the field that make Allen proud to call him a friend.

"I've come to know him better over the years," Allen says. "There are some people who are just memorable. Lem is like a light on a hill for everybody to see. I think it's because of his energy, spirituality, and presence. If you're alive and conscious, you cannot help but notice it. He always has a kind word to say, and his words are backed by love."

Allen says that he and Lem occasionally talk about sports, but they mostly talk about life. "Football is what we did, but it's not who we are. I remember Lem the person more than I remember Lem the player."

Lem also has an opinion as to what makes a hero. "A hero is a person who accepts the responsibilities of divine nature through God, not necessarily a sports figure," he says. "Heroes create motivation, insight, and kindness, and take it to the next level. The human spirit motivates to go higher." Lem looks to his parents as heroes and mentors, but he says that the ultimate hero is Christ. "He is the undefeated warrior," Lem says. "He's a great motivator and my source of inspiration. He followed the path of success."

Lem finds his comfort zone within the scriptures. They prevent him from "edging God out." One of his greatest sources of inspiration and guidance comes from *Luke, 9:23*. "If anyone will come after me, he must deny himself, pick up his cross daily, and follow me," Lem says. "*Ego* is Edging God Out. You can't gratify yourself. Instead, deny yourself and don't always think of yourself as more important than you are. Confidence is different because you're in step with God and the Commandments. It is an assuredness in the way you deal with that."

Lem checks his ego at the door as he attempts to get into God's Hall of Fame, but admits that there were moments in his life when he forgot this formula for true success. "There were times during those years that I thought I was alone on the football field," he says. "But it is He who is in you and He who is the world. *(John 4:4)*.

"You dear children are from God and have overcome life's difficulties because the One who is in you is greater than the one in the world. It was the One who was in us that propelled us to do it. I had to give up the, 'I am wonderful' attitude. It is the One inside you—the spirit that helps you manifest those great things."

While performing his magic on the gridiron, Lem had ample opportunity to celebrate in a showy way. Today, he is encouraged when he sees players thanking God for their success in celebration. "Some in the media don't like players who rejoice, offer prayers, and pay homage to the Lord," Lem says. "At the Hall of Fame reunion, I was asked what it's like watching the game today and witnessing players pump their chest and look up and thank the Lord. My answer is always the same—I think it's great." To Lem, there is no bad time to pray. And wherever and whenever one prays, that's where your church is housed.

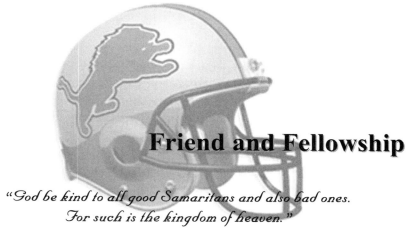

Friend and Fellowship

"God be kind to all good Samaritans and also bad ones.
For such is the kingdom of heaven."

—*John Gardner*

𝓘T IS ONE OF THE SHIPS THAT LEM BARNEY often rides during the storms. Storms he knows life will bring. For him, fellowship is not done reluctantly. It is something done with a giving heart. Giving with his heart and teaching the Word through fellowship is something Lem thrives on. He derives great joy from sharing coffee or a meal while discussing scriptures. The Word is with Lem always, and he is always with the Word.

"The Lord demands that you be strong and courageous—not terrified or discouraged," he says. "'For I, the Lord your God, will be with you wherever you go.' If we do the things that God has asked us to do, He will do the things that He has promised that He will do for us."

Lem seeks His way when engaged in simple daily routines and finds the method to pray in unconventional ways. "While driving, I use the SCHOOL acronym," he says. "To me it represents Salvation Comes Heavenly Out Of Love, and on our streets you can turn right or left." The STOP sign to Lem is "Shout Thanks Of Praise."

"The Holy Spirit lives in His Word," Lem says. "When I'm in my car, I pray for thanks and thanksgiving. And if you want to know what a miracle is, it is getting from point A to point B without incident. Prayer is an important item of my daily ritual. Just like breathing, it's an act of motion and meditation.

Lem believes that the Lord has given us a way back to Him—and it is through His son. "If you love me, you will keep my commandments," He said. These directives are not mere suggestions. They're the proofs that show Him each day that we are following His commandments. You can fool some of the people some of the time and a lot of the people a lot of the time, but we cannot fool God any time. Our relationship with the Lord is based not on a feeling, but on understanding and knowledge. "Be still and you can experience God," Lem says. "We are truly saved with the knowledge of God."

Over the years, Reverend Barney's approach to nonbelievers has evolved. "I used to be confrontational with the dogmatic person," he says. "But discussing faith should not be an argument or a debate. You share your knowledge with gentleness, kindness, and understanding.

"I explain to people in a loving manner what the Lord has accomplished in our lives. I believe that confrontation only hardens people and is counterproductive to the goal of education. When you present all the evidence in support of God's remarkable impact and influence on our lives,," he says, "people will quickly come to the side of the Lord."

In his younger years, Lem tried to win football games. Now he tries to win souls.

"Since being ordained, the greatest achievements of my life have changed from Hall of Fame awards to soldiering for the Lord," Lem says. "I love to do all the things that Christ has asked me to do. By reading his Word, He communicates to me. I can wait for the Spirit to guide me in all truth."

For three years, Lem served as area director of the Fellowship of Christian Athletes of Southeast Michigan. While at the FCA, Lem was responsible for setting up huddle prayer groups in grade schools, high schools, and colleges within the school's curriculum in a way to reach all denominations and to teach Jesus in the public school systems.

The program had meetings before and after school to help student-athletes grow spiritually. "Because it was a Bible study within a group of student athletes, it was a real joy for me to assemble with them." Many of the student-athletes that Lem worked with weren't regular church-goers. Many of their parents did not insist that their children participate in church. "As a result," Lem says, "when I see these previously non-involved students begin to receive the message that will bring peace and joy to their lives with the Holy Spirit and God, I'm very proud.

"People seem to search for popular movements to become involved with, but for me, the greatest movement in life is a movement toward Christ. Be obedient and have a lifelong relationship with the Lord," he says. "We are charged to love the Lord with all of our heart, and we must also love our neighbor as we love ourselves."

Jerry Green remembers Lem's fellowship ways as a player. "He was very religious," Green says. "I've attended dinners at which he was asked to deliver the benediction. He always agreed and demonstrated to the group the depth of his faith. On a personal side, when my wife was very sick and had been for a long time, Lem would often call her on the phone just to lift her spirits." Green's wife passed away in 2002, but Green says he'll always remember the heartfelt prayers that Lem offered during those tough times.

Mel Blount believes that he and Lem sail together on the two most important ships—fellowship and friendship. "We have something in common," Blount says. "And what we have in common is that we're men of God and we are strong believers." It is their faith and their hope that keeps them going. "You cannot define a person only by what they do," Blount says. "Longfellow once wrote that 'the world judges us by what we have done, while we judge ourselves by what we feel capable of doing.' The difference is our outside versus our inside. When evaluating very successful people, it's hard to find a difference between the heart and the soul. Lem Barney is one of those people."

Benny White won't ever forget the dual blessings that Lem has brought to his life. "Lem taught me to live life with enthusiasm and with love," White says. "Most importantly, he taught me to have a relationship with the Lord. He showed me his life example. Sometimes, I call him and remind him of just that. And I thank him for introducing me and helping me understand the importance of how to live with the Lord."

Detroit Pistons great Dave Bing goes back a long way with Lem. Theirs is a friendship that goes beyond the sports headlines and the parties. Both men speak of each as brothers.

"He's still 'Mr. Piston' as far as I'm concerned," Lem says. "We first met during my rookie year. The two of us have now become closer than biological brothers." Bing was a star ballplayer when the Pistons were struggling, just as Lem was with the Lions. This helped forge a great bond between them. "Dave met my mom and dad, and he was there when I lost them," Lem says. "I share a fellowship with Dave, and he's an active member at Hartford Memorial Church."

Another man Lem shares friendship and fellowship with is his former Jackson State teammate Joe Hoskins. "When we played ball back then in a pickup game, I thought I was a pretty good athlete, but I could see right away that Lem was something out of the ordinary," says Hoskins, who looked his friend up when he first got to Detroit. "I had no job when I arrived in Detroit, and Lem took me in and provided for me."

Hoskins says he's never seen an athlete as kind or as generous as Lem. But when they played the game, Lem would knock his opponents down the way he was trained. "During one game," Hoskins says, "I remember Lem helping Gayle Sayers get up after he'd hit him. I did not take kindly to it. I didn't think Lem should have used his energy to help an opponent, even if they had been in the same fraternity. But Lem's motto was 'kill 'em with kindness.'"

Through the years, Lem has relied on finding, forming, and maintaining solid relationships that would help when the storms came. He recently talked about their importance to a group of friends who had gathered to honor him.

"While I am an ordained minister," he told them, "I will not preach a sermon today. But if today's text had a theme, it would be, 'Are you maintaining your ships for the storms that are going to come in your life?' Remember that in life, we are either in a storm, coming out of a storm, or see a storm approaching. Therefore, we all need to prepare and maintain our ships.

"Keep in mind," he said, "that when you're going through a storm or see one coming, you need good friends, good fellowships, and good relationships to help get you through."

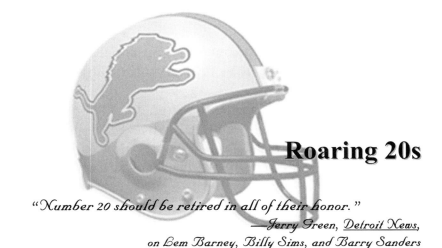

Roaring 20s

"Number 20 should be retired in all of their honor."
—Jerry Green, Detroit News,
on Lem Barney, Billy Sims, and Barry Sanders

SOME NUMBERS IN SPORTS ARE SPECIAL. In baseball, Number 3 means The Babe, and Number 24 means Willie Mays, the Say Hey Kid. In hockey, Number 9 means Mr. Hockey, Gordie Howe, while Number 99 will always belong to Wayne Gretzky. In basketball, Number 23 will forever be associated with Michael Jordan. Meanwhile in football, at least in Detroit, Number 20 remains a magical and mystical double digit.

To Lions fans, Number 20 means three things, three names, and three players who have, above all, one thing in common—greatness.

Lem, Billy, and Barry.

Before 1967, the number was worn by 12 other Lions players: Grover Emerson (1934-37), James A. McDonald (1938-40), Bert Kuczinski (1943), Elvin Liles (1943-45), Lloyd Wickett (1943,1946), Richard Weber (1945), Ted Cook (1947), Lawrence Ellis (1948), Daniel Sandifer (1950), William Stits (1954-56), Jim Steffen (1959-60), and Dick Compton (1962-64).

Unlike Lem, Billy, and Barry, these players weren't exactly household names and certainly not famous enough to be acknowledged by the mere mention of their names. But you hardly needed a last name with Barney, Sims, or Sanders, and you never needed a program to identify their greatness. While the rest of the world considered 10 to be the best you could be, Lions fans knew that 20 signified perfection in a football player.

Music to the ears of Detroit football fans everywhere, Lem Barney, Billy Sims, and Barry Sanders were all special players with a common number. They dazzled, dashed, and delivered excellence on the football field from 1967 to 1998, all signified by that same special number on their jerseys.

It generated a very unique brand of 20-20 vision on the field at both Tiger Stadium and later at the Pontiac Silverdome. The picture was always crystal-clear. While the Super Bowl title never arrived, Detroiters came to count on excellence from the three great Lions who shared the same number. Each Sunday, they would always count on these roaring 20s to deliver something wonderful between the lines.

Lem empathizes with Barry Sanders and can relate all too well to what the last great Number 20 experienced—and to the circumstances that ultimately contributed to his early retirement.

"I tried to provide support for Barry while the Lions continued to languish in the standings," Lem says. "Barry was doing his job, but it just wasn't the right time in history for all of his hard work to be fully recognized. Usually, when a coach felt that a change is needed and a player's services were no longer required, the player would receive that news directly from the coach. However, in Barry's situation, the roles were reversed, as he removed himself from the game. Barry thought it was time to go. He had lost his passion for the game."

Jerry Green covered each of these legendary Number 20s and believes that the mighty threesome deserve the honor of seeing their number retired. Sims, the man who inherited the number from Lem, is excited by this idea. "It's an honor for all of us," he says. "When I finally had the opportunity to meet Lem Barney, I was pleased and privileged. The things he had accomplished for the Detroit Lions were impressive, and I was honored to later be able to wear that special number. Unlike Lem, however, I wore the number 20 through high school and college as well."

Sims felt it was only appropriate that the digits he and Lem made famous be passed on to Sanders, who, like Sims, won college football's Heisman Trophy. "I've known Barry since his college days," Sims says. "When I learned that he was going to wear the same number I wore, I knew a lot of great things were going to come from him. It was an honor for me to see him share it.

"I remember when Barry was drafted. [Lions coach] Wayne Fontes came from Tampa and scouted him personally. The Lions were trying to decide between Barry and Deion [Sanders]. I called Wayne and told him he'd be crazy not to draft Barry because of the potential impact he could make on the team."

The Lions made great draft choices in these three roaring 20s. Each entered the NFL with a bang and never looked back.

"My first game against the Rams set the pace for the way I wanted to be remembered," Sims says. "When I was going through training camp, I didn't really show too much. I was learning on the job in preseason games. Then, in my first pro game in Anaheim, I ran for 157 yards and scored three touchdowns. That set the stage for what I wanted to do in the NFL. And in spite of the team's lack of success, hopefully the fans will remember that when I was on the field, I gave it my all."

The frustration from never making it to the Super Bowl didn't affect Sims' play on the field. "I never spoke to Barry or Lem about that," Sims says. "You can tell looking back that it was frustrating. Even with all the talent and skills we possessed, I realized it still takes a team effort to rise to that level. The closest I ever came was our last-minute [playoff] loss to San Francisco [in 1983]. We were two games from getting to the Super Bowl. It was very frustrating, but I wouldn't trade it for anything."

After a serious knee injury in 1984, Sims had to face possible retirement. "I had a setback when I tried to start an offensive move too quickly," he says. "Perhaps I could've come back, but I would have been a totally different type of runner. I chose not to do that. It was best for me to hang it up."

Sims remains proud to be included in this all-star trio of Number 20s. "Lem played when the Lions were at Tiger Stadium and subject to all that cold weather," he says. "By comparison, we had it pretty good playing inside the Silverdome. Lem's work ethic impressed me. I knew that every time he was on the field, his opponents were worried about him. My hat goes off to him for the great success he achieved and how he approached his job."

And when it comes to Barry Sanders, words alone cannot describe the things he was able to do on the field. "He remains a star ambassador for the Lions," Sims says. "What kids can learn from those two guys is how to carry yourself and how to pay proper respect for the players and the game."

The thought of retiring Number 20 also pleases Sanders. Recently inducted into the Pro Football Hall of Fame, Sanders speaks from his heart on how he came to know Lem, the original 20. "Before coming to Detroit, I had never heard of Lem Barney," Sanders admits. "During my first year, we met and he introduced himself to me. Mostly, what I knew about Lem was through other players and fans. As a big Oklahoma fan, I often watched Billy Sims play and was familiar with him. But in Detroit, people were quick to tell me about Lem Barney."

His first meeting with Lem created a memorable first impression. "His main focus of conversation was not about his football career," Sanders says. "Before games, Lem would come into the locker room and offer encouraging words, but always ending with his admonition to go out there and have fun and play your game. Those words made an impression on me. Of course, I later learned from all the others that he had been a fantastic player himself."

Sanders quickly discovered more about Lem, especially his passion for his fellow man. "Lem's love for and appreciation of life is truly contagious," Sanders says. "He always builds a person up and is really concerned about their welfare. One thing that he always cautioned me about was making sure that I would be able to have a nice life after football. That is indeed the person I know as Lem Barney—concerned that others were doing well emotionally, spiritually, and professionally."

Lem and Barry have never spoken at length about their similar lack of team success with the Lions, but Sanders recognizes that they share a kinship. "Lem understood what I was experiencing and going through with the team," he says. "He would always tell me to hang in there, that things are going to be okay. They'll get better."

Former New York Giants star Frank Gifford witnessed the exploits of all the roaring 20s from his perch in ABC's "Monday Night Football" booth. "My son is a big Barry Sanders fan," he says. "We went to see Barry inducted into the Hall of Fame, and Lem Barney was there. We managed to spend some pleasant time with Lem. My son was totally charmed."

During a delay at the induction ceremony, Gifford asked Lem to go up and give the invocation. "Do you think I should?" Lem asked. Gifford replied that of course he should—and so he did. "Quite frankly," Gifford says, "he gave the best speech of the entire program."

Two of the three great Detroit Lion Number 20s share a place in the same Hall of Fame, an honor that Sanders does not take it lightly. "It made a great impact on me," Sanders says. "It sets you apart from most players. To rub shoulders with the individuals from every era who really shaped…the game is a very special and unique experience. I never made it to the Super Bowl."

Like Lem, Sanders has always been a fan of the game that he mastered. "The first guy I saw who had an impact on me was Terry Metcalf from the [St. Louis] Cardinals," he says. "I was always one of the smaller guys on the field, so I related to guys like him, especially the running backs. I was always a big fan of the game."

Sanders is the first to admit he doesn't understand what it is that makes some players special. "It's hard to put a finger on it exactly," he says. "I don't know why I reacted a certain way on the field when a different player may have chosen some other response. Those are things I just don't have an answer for."

Sanders seems to imply that those all-star reactions of Lem and other Hall of Famers seem to be intuitive and deep-rooted. "For opposing teams, Lem was a dangerous player," he says. "But he is also a remarkable individual. I know he has certain intangible qualities within, qualities some people may not even think are necessary to make a great football player. But it was those great qualities that allowed him to excel at everything he tried."

Those same qualities rooted within Lem are also deep-rooted in Sanders. "My dad had a tendency to present a stoic image," he says, "but I know that deep inside, he was tickled to death that his son became one of the best running backs in the NFL."

Although he retired early, Sanders harbors no regrets. "There was nothing equal to strapping on that helmet," he says. "In many ways, the game helped me discover what I was made of. Things didn't always go the way I wanted them to go, but still I managed to keep fighting and scrapping. I came into the league with an attitude that required me to carry my load and to do everything I could to be the best player I was able to be."

It's a philosophy that Sanders preaches and seems to echo Lem's own philosophy. "When I was in high school, I wanted to be the best high school player," Sanders says. "When I was in college, I wanted to be the best college player. Whatever level you're playing at, be the best that you can be. Learn as much as you can about the game, because that's how you become a good player at the next level, whatever that level may be."

The next level in Sanders' life is yet to be determined. Still, one thing is certain—the most recent Lions Number 20 will always hold the original Number 20 in high regard. "I'll remember Lem Barney as a person who deeply cares about people," Sanders says. "He's more concerned with the type of man that he is than the type of stats he put up. He happened to be a very, very good football player. A lot of people think he came years before his time. He was a terrific athlete and a solid human being. Lem had the good fortune to have a mom and dad who encouraged their son to work hard, to stand out and to be unique and not afraid to be excellent."

Sanders looks to Lem for inspiration down the road, too. "I hope that when I'm out of the game for as long as he's been, that I'm as productive and helpful to everyone around me. If that happens, I would've made the adjustment to life after football and can be the type of family man, and as effective in my community as he is."

It's for these reasons that all of the roaring 20s believe seeing their number hanging from the rafters at Ford Field would be a splendid testimonial. "Retiring the old number 20 will be good for the Lions organization, its football history, the fans, and our state," Sims says. "I learned early in Detroit just how much the whole city and state loves its sports teams. If Detroit ever wins a Super Bowl, the state of Michigan will have to close for the celebration."

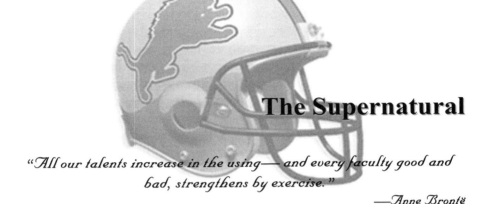

The Supernatural

"All our talents increase in the using— and every faculty good and bad, strengthens by exercise."

—Anne Brontë

WHERE DOES TALENT COME FROM? ARE great salesmen made, or are they born? Where does an artist get his inspiration? How does he make it look so easy? How does an athlete do those things with such grace? Is it hard work, practice, discipline, or more?

Do any of these explanations fully describe the extraordinary performance by the gifted singer, the graceful dancer, the passionate painter, or the skilled athlete?

Where do they get their gifts? Is it a God-given ability? How does one describe the talents of a unique athlete such as Lem Barney? Only one word seems to apply—supernatural. It was because of Lem's graceful athleticism that Jerry Green first dubbed him The Supernatural. "He was a natural athlete, spectacular and flamboyant." Green says. "He was one of the hot dogs before it became fashionable. But the manner in which Lem did it was not objectionable, unlike the way some players do today."

Lem brought his supernatural abilities to all aspects of his being. "Lem was probably the most all-around gifted athlete I had ever been around," says Charlie Sanders. "I mean he could play scratch golf and never took a lesson ... tennis, basketball ... just a natural athlete. He could do anything, and it was no struggle for him. He was smooth. That stood out about him, just how natural and graceful he was."

"Lem is the best all-around athlete that I have ever seen," says Dave Bing. "He can play anything—golf, tennis, softball, swim, and even bowl. He is a total athlete."

The legends of the game immediately recognize abilities in certain players that are not shared by all of their contemporaries. "Players cannot be taught the attributes of a great player," says Gale Sayers. "No one taught me how to run with the football. Nobody taught me how to see the whole field. These were God-given abilities. Good players don't make it to the NFL. It requires a person with God-given talent. We saw that in Lem."

Sayers says that Lem was quick and that he quickly recognized plays. He was bound to be a Hall of Famer. "Off the field, Lem has always been a good guy. When he first came into the league, he had the type of personality that you gravitated toward. He always had a smile on his face. We had a few battles on the field during our time, but every time he would land on top of me, he would help me up."

On the football field, it seemed there was nothing Lem couldn't do except sit on the bench. "I could play both sides of the ball and played wide receiver the first three seasons," Lem says. "On occasion, I would be left in the game after punt returns. As a former quarterback, I knew about routes and running patterns. As a defensive back, you have to run efficiently because a wide receiver runs his pattern forward. However, as a receiver, I was not as effective as Deion Sanders."

Lem's opponents believe that his greatness grew because it was matched by an equal portion of dedication. "The difference between good and great comes when a player is willing to pay the price," says Hall of Fame defensive back Kenny Houston. "Lem paid the price on the practice field and early in his career at Jackson State. Having played in the Southwestern Athletic Conference, Lem's work ethic was outstanding and was recognized by those small black colleges. His conditioning and effort were second to none."

Even when the games didn't matter in the standings, such as an exhibition game in North Carolina against the Washington Redskins, Lem always showed up with his A game.

"Lem was playing safety in a punt situation," Green says. "He got the ball on the Lions' 40, cut to his right and outran everybody. At about the 10-yard line, he turned around and waved at the two Redskins chasing him. He gave them a little goodbye wave. If anybody else had done that, they would have been criticized for taunting and showing off. But with Lem, it came so naturally and seemed so normal. I think he knew that he was pretty good and I still think he knows it."

If he had to do it all over again, Lem says he wouldn't change much. "Looking back now, it seemed so easy," he says. "I wanted to become a pro football player. I realized that dream. I tell people that if the Lord has given you those gifts and talents, then He expects you to use them."

Lem says he has no regrets about his football career. But knowing what he knows now, what would he do differently? "I would choose to play either golf or tennis," he says. "In either of those professional sports, your professional career is nearly unlimited and your final results don't depend on the efforts of a team. I love both of these games and play them trying to duplicate the techniques of the professionals I watch."

And no one doubts that Lem would've been a world-class golf or tennis pro.

Jerry Green was right. Supernatural indeed.

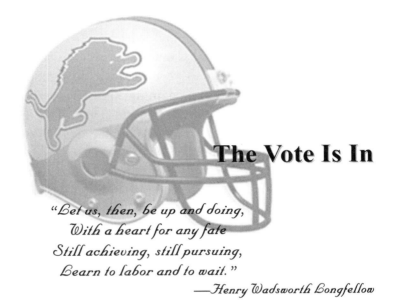

The Vote Is In

"Let us, then, be up and doing,
With a heart for any fate
Still achieving, still pursuing,
Learn to labor and to wait."

—Henry Wadsworth Longfellow

THERE ARE FEW CLUBS WITH A MORE exclusive membership than the Pro Football Hall of Fame in Canton, Ohio. The names of its members take your breath away: Unitas, Sayers, Montana, Brown, Jones, Griese, Payton, and Starr.

To be a member, you must have been a star—a star that shined bright and long. A star that shined more brightly that 99.9 percent of all the men who have ever worn a uniform. In the long history of the National Football League, thousands of players have played the game, but fewer than 200 of them are enshrined in the Hall.

For Lem Barney, the Hall of Fame wasn't something he thought a lot about. He prides himself on thinking only about the game and the results that he could control on game day. "I was always trying to put my best foot forward and never dreamt about winning awards or entering the Hall of Fame," he says. "The very idea of the Hall of Fame did not dawn on me for several years until after my retirement.

"I played with a guy named Walt Williams. In his rookie year with the Lions in 1977, he began calling me a Hall of Famer. It was just a nice compliment he was paying me that ended up becoming a reality. The next time I can remember the subject coming up was when Jerry Green brought it up. Green was then one of the 15 sportswriters from the Detroit area who had a Hall of Fame vote."

To win induction, a candidate must receive about ninety percent of the overall vote. The first year Lem was eligible for consideration was 1991, but the process of gaining induction could take as few as four or as many as seven players. In 1991, four candidates were inducted into the Hall. "If they would have gone with five new inductees," Green told Lem, "you would have been in."

Having narrowly missed election into this most elite of clubs, Lem didn't dwell on it. "I had hopes that it would happen, but I didn't fall apart when I missed out," he says. "It just was not my time that year."

The following year, Lem was again notified that he was being considered. He took the nomination in stride as he worked on his stroke at the 1992 Super Bowl Golf Classic.

"I wasn't setting high expectations," he says. "I was playing golf for the Warner Lambert Pharmaceutical Company during Super Bowl weekend in Miami. It was the final round of nominations for Hall of Fame balloting, and as I came off the course into the clubhouse, I ran into Bryant Gumbel."

"Have you heard any news yet," Bryant asked.

"No," said Lem. "I haven't heard anything yet, but I'm going to my room to check." He was hoping there would be a message waiting for him.

"As I unlocked my hotel room door, the telephone was ringing," Lem says. "It was Jerry Green on the phone. 'Lem Barney, the Supernatural,' he said. 'Congratulations! You are a Hall of Famer!'"

Green remembers Lem's entry into the Hall of Fame. "I had to speak on his behalf the day he was elected," he says. "His failure to make it the first time around was no surprise. Most nominees don't make it. I felt a sense of pride as I was speaking on his behalf. I was helping a guy to be inducted into the Pro Football Hall of Fame, while not cheering for him."

The pride that Green felt was because he had watched Lem come up to stardom in the NFL from an unknown black school in Mississippi. "That pride was justifiable," Green says, "and the honoring of Lem Barney was overdue."

For Lem, the news left him in a reflective mood. "In retrospect," he says, "my induction into the Hall of Fame was the result of a combination of things. The fact that for most of my career, I had been a multi-purpose player—a punt and kick return specialist, as well as cornerback—probably helped. I had God-given physical skills of speed and quickness. I was a finesse player with an astute nose for the ball. I liked to get my offense in good field position." Lem had run for 1,077 yards, the highest average (19.2 yards) for a defensive back, and had racked up 56 interceptions.

"At the awards ceremony," Lem says, "I was asked if this recognition was a dream come true. I've said before that while I was playing, I did not think of awards or professional accolades. My only focus was on helping my teams win. While you're busy playing in the league, there's little time to dream of the NFL's Hall of Fame. My dream was to become the very best football player I could be."

Lem's day of recognition was one that left memories swirling through his mind. "The Hall of Fame ceremonies were sheer drama," he says. "You reflect back on all of the coaches that you've played for and all the opponents you've faced. You remember all the work and sacrifice that Mom and Dad made to make sure that I arrived at school and practice on time. It was a period of great reflection."

The Hall

THE DAY ARRIVED, A SUMMER DAY IN August when the most distinguished players of the National Football League are enshrined into the hallowed halls of professional football in Canton, Ohio. A day bigger than description, a day the man from Gulfport never dreamed would come. "You dream about playing football in the pros, but to even imagine induction into the Hall of Fame was too big to comprehend," Lem says.

On this day in 1992, it was Lem's time. This is where his footsteps across all the football fields of his life had led, to the final steps into the Professional Football Hall of Fame.

"My wife and children accompanied me on the trip," Lem says, recalling that eventful three-day journey to Canton. "We arrived early to participate in pre-induction ceremonies. On Saturday, a parade kicked off the program and the full reality of this honor was brought home. It was an adrenaline-filled day, and I was joined by the four other inductees—Deacon Jones, John Riggins, John Mackey, and Al Davis."

It was Jones who spoke about the qualities that make Hall of Fame club members different. "Commitment and hard work are the standards that set the greats apart from the rest," he said. "Those are the attributes that made Lem and his group of inductees so special. Sitting next to the best of the best, a bond naturally develops. No jealousy or memories of old injuries lay between us. We are now NFL Hall of Famers, a feeling unlike any other, joining the club where the best of the best reside."

For wide receiver Don Maynard of the New York Jets, Lem's enshrinement in the Hall of Fame represents both justice and sadness. "Everyone in the Hall of Fame deserves to be there, and Lem is one of the greatest corners to play the game," he says. "All of the present Hall of Famers are dedicated players who deserved the award. I'm just disappointed that some of the guys I thought deserved to be there were not inducted."

"The Hall of Fame is the ultimate honor," says Mel Blount. "My joy is in the people I met, the accomplishments, the Super Bowl, and the friendships that we made for life. I really cherish those things."

Some memberships come with privileges, but membership in the Hall of Fame is considered a privilege by everyone honored with induction. "The Hall of Fame club is a very small fraternity," Gale Sayers says. "Once you're in, it becomes a brotherhood, a family. I go back every year to see the greats who helped to build this game. About 100 of us come back every year."

Today, Sayers thinks that too many kids don't know their NFL history. "Kids don't know who Dick Butkus or Jim Brown are," he says. "Football fans must realize that if it weren't for those people in the past—living or dead—there would not be an NFL today. I visit the annual induction ceremonies to let newcomers know that there was somebody who came before them. I always enjoy my time there and usually have an opportunity to spend a bit of quality time with Lem."

While the game has changed, it remains a national pastime only because of the great players who have dedicated themselves to excellence. "Skilled players like the Lem Barneys are just as needed today," says former Dallas Cowboys quarterback Roger Staubach. "You don't have to be bigger, stronger, or faster than anyone else;

you only need to be as committed to the game as players like Gale Sayers, Jimmy Brown, Walter Payton, and Lem Barney were."

There's a thread of excellence that runs through every member. "The common denominator is heart," Staubach says. "I don't think you're inducted into the Hall unless you had a fierce passion inside of you. Most NFL players have a great deal of talent, but there are a lot of players with talent who aren't in the Hall of Fame. The Hall of Famer has utilized that talent, tremendous resiliency, perseverance, and heart to further his goal."

It's a club founded on exclusivity. "The Hall is supposed to be pure, based on pure talent," Kenny Houston says. "Even though Lem did not play on winning teams, he was a winning individual."

The great players are also students of the game, respecting those who came before them, and offering insight to those who follow. "Anytime you play a sport like football," says former San Francisco 49ers defensive back Ronnie Lott, "there are people you look up to as role models. Growing up, you looked up to those people, whether it was the president of the United States or the pastor in your church, not because of who they are so much as what they had accomplished."

Lott says that if you reach the pinnacle that your role model has, you also gain an understanding of what level of skill, talent, and commitment is required. "I've shared experiences with guys like Lem Barney, Dick "Night Train" Lane, Ken Houston, Mike Haynes, and a lot of other great football players," he says. "There's something special about trying to emulate your heroes, trying to be a part of their club. And should you be successful, it becomes the ultimate compliment."

Lem remembers the weekend he was welcomed into this elite fraternity. "The importance of the place was emphasized at a very special luncheon that Ray Nitschke, until his death, presided over," Lem says. The Hall of Fame luncheon is held the day after the parade and is open only to Hall of Fame members and staff. Members of this exclusive club usually say a few words of congratulations, pointing out that the new members were now part of a team where teammates could not be cut or traded.

Hall of Famers are expected to set a good example to the league and to the world. "You now represent the club that represents the best of the best," Lem says, "and your public behavior should demonstrate that."

Lem Barney exudes class. And as a member of the Class of '92, he was thrilled to see many of his Lions teammates make the trip down to Canton to pay tribute to him. Forty-seven former Lions showed up to help honor their friend—all of them adorned in Lem Barney T-shirts and Lem Barney derbies. Mel Farr, Mike Lucci, Mike Weger, and Pat Studstill came all the way from California. Tommy Watkins and many others were also on hand. "What a great feeling to have all of the guys who sweated, bled, and shared tears with there," Lem says. "We were together when we won and when we lost, and while we were fighting the good fight. That was a joy and camaraderie I don't think I'll ever realize again."

Weger remembers surprising Lem on that Hall of Fame weekend. "We had taken a room with a bunch of the guys, and Lem had no idea that all of us would be there," he says. "We loved to get together, tell funny stories, and just hang out. When Lem arrived and discovered us, he was truly elated that we had taken the time to share this moment with him."

Lem remembers the man assigned to drive him in the Hall of Fame parade. The driver, a man named Spence, told Lem that the people were going crazy over his induction.

"Are you ready with a speech?" he asked Lem.

Lem told him that his speeches were always unrehearsed and from the heart.

"Okay," said Spence, "but do you have any questions about how the program will be conducted?"

"Well, Spence," said Lem, "I was wondering if it would be appropriate for me to sing."

"Well," Spence replied, "this is your day and you should do exactly what you want to."

It was customary for the inductee to pick a person who would act as his official presenter. When they asked Lem who he would like to present him, he asked that his old friend and teammate Jimmy David handle that responsibility.

"Jimmy was my friend, a great motivator, great tactician, great instructor, and a great teacher," Lem says. "Those skills that Jimmy had instilled in me were in part responsible for my induction into the Hall of Fame."

As the clock ran down toward the induction, Lem looked within for answers. "Unlike most people, I did not speak from notes," he says. "The first day we arrived in Canton, I looked at myself in the mirror and realized that this program was going to be an emotional affair. I asked myself if it would be all right if I cried. Would it be acceptable for me to be standing in front of the tough football world with tears all over my face?"

Lem decided that crying might be okay, so long as he had a towel stashed in his pocket. "I kept that face towel during all of the events that week and it did not go unused," he says.

Deacon Jones and some of the other players were becoming very emotional. The scene was becoming nearly as exciting for Lem as a kickoff. "It had been a long time since I had been a rookie in the NFL, but this experience was the same—a rookie entering the Hall of Fame.

Lem remembers the big day that was beautifully accented by his little girl singing for her daddy. "During the ceremonies, it was a real joy hearing my 18-year-old daughter Latrece sing the national anthem," he says. "She really kicked it all off beautifully. And then my coach Jimmy David spoke. It seems like just yesterday that I heard his kind introduction."

"Thank you very much," David said on the podium. "I'm very proud to be here today on what people call football's greatest weekend. I am also honored that Lem Barney has asked me to say a few words on his behalf. Players of his kind come around once in a lifetime, and I feel fortunate that I had the opportunity to coach him. But this is truly Lem Barney's greatest weekend in football, a fitting cap to a spectacular career in football.

"When Lem Barney played for Joe Schmidt and myself, I hadn't seen an athlete so talented and as a pro football player, he had all of the qualifications—speed, quickness, great hands and that necessary

combination of brains, guts, and love. Lem played the most difficult, demanding positions. He played cornerback, punt returner, kickoff returner, and was a backup punter.

"The first game he ever played in the NFL, he picked off Super Bowl champ Bart Starr's pass and ran it in for a touchdown. That same season, he allowed only one touchdown pass all year and he was named defensive rookie of the year, went on to seven Pro Bowls, had eleven career touchdowns and 56 career interceptions.

"Lem Barney was simply a natural and is a true champion. But the stats don't give you the whole picture. It seems some players today think of football as an individual sport. Lem never forgot that football was a team sport. On the sidelines or in the locker room, he was just as valuable to our team as he was on the field. He never failed to lend a helping hand, or give advice, or take advantage of a situation to help raise the morale of our team and our level of play. All of this is so important today because Hall of Famers are positive role models who must exude championship qualities on and off the field.

Lem made a lasting impression on me ... and is still in the business of making lasting impressions on people through his work with countless community and charitable organizations. The kids of Special Olympics know him, the kids of Children's Hospital know him, The United Way, Easter Seals, The United Negro College Fund, and the Boy Scouts of America know him. Lem Barney gave back and continues to give back much more than he ever took from football.

"And after today, all of you will know him a little better, too. A very special guy, flamboyant, a lot of fun to be with, and today the name 'Lem Barney' goes down [in] history as he joins Willie Brown, Herb Adderley, Night Train Lane, and Mel Blount as only the fifth cornerback to be enshrined. This adds to his many accolades, the Detroit Lions Hall of Fame, the Michigan Hall of Fame, and now the highest honor of all, the Professional Football Hall of Fame. We used to have a saying that the losers look at the stats and the winners look at the scoreboard. Lem, you're still looking at the scoreboard.

"Ladies and gentleman, no one that I've ever coached is more deserving of this high honor than this man, my player, and my friend, Lem Barney.

222

With David's introduction, it was Lem's turn to step up to the microphone.

"Thank you very much, Coach Jimmy David. Before I start a presentation, if we will, I'd like to just take a silent moment of prayer before the greatest men that have ever strutted on the field that measured 100 yards by 53 yards ... to remember that this year, we lost four fallen heroes from these halls: Mel Hein, Alex Wojciechowicz, the late, great Paul Brown, and as of recent, Buck Buchanan. Let's just give a few minutes of silence for them. Thank You.

"This is my crying towel—just in case I need it."

Just then, Lem began to sing.

"For once in a lifetime, a man knows a moment, one wonderful moment, when fate takes his hand."

Overcome by emotion, Lem paused in mid-song …

"I won't finish," he said.

"But this is my moment and I am most pleased and fortunate that you're here to share it with me. I've said all along for many years, success, accomplishments, and achievements are no good unless you have someone that you love to share it with. And today you share it with me.

"To the presenter of these great men, to the fellow Hall of Famers, to the class of '92, to their wonderful families, to my families, to my legions of fans, to my throngs of supporters, and to my multitude of well-wishers. Today, if I had something to leave as a message, it would be of thanks and gratitude and all involving love. Thanks to my family for the support that's been rendered not only through the good times, but as well through the bad times. Most grateful to the eternal for the God-given skills, talents, and attributes that I was given. To have played the game that I dreamed of and to play in the National Football League. To my mom and dad, who are not here physically, but I know they're here spiritually.

"My mom and dad, who are my role models, my heroes, and my mentors. To my friends, more importantly, to my teammates from the sandlots, to prep school, to collegiate ball and to the National

Football League. Thank you for your encouragement, for your support, for your motivation.

"Life does not always deal us fair hands, but the hands that life deals us—we must play them. We must play the game of life in order to win and win at all costs. No one ever dreams of getting to this spot once he comes into the National Football League. If anyone ever dreams of getting into the Hall of Fame, he's having a nightmare. One dreams of being able to utilize his talents, skills, and attributes to make them manifest, to make them fruits. I believe mine were manifested.

"Football for me for 20 years was a way of life. I enjoyed it, I whistled while I worked, and every opportunity I had, I tried to promote victories and wins. Life has been good to me, and if I died tonight I wouldn't die blue because I've experienced some very great things in life.

"Love, I believe, is our most motivating factor that we can have in life. Love for self, love for God, love for team, and love for friends, love for our co-workers, and love for our community and country. Love, our most powerful weapon. It was once said that love is the only game in town that's not called off because of darkness. Love is so powerful.

"I'd like to culminate my acceptance by rendering what I believe is the world's greatest love song ever written, penned by one of the world's greatest lexicologists, by a great disciple. It's brother Paul. It comes from Corinthians 1:13 and it simply states, 'Though I speak with the tongues of men and angels, and I have not loved, I have become a sounding brass or a twinkling symbol, though I have the gift of prophesies to understand all mysteries and understand all knowledge and have all faith so that I can remove mountains and have not loved, I am nothing.

"'Though I bestow all goods to feed the poor, though I give my body to be burned and have not love, it prophets me nothing. For love is long suffering, but love is kind. Love is envieth not, love wanteth not and love is not all puffed up. Love does not behave itself unseemingly, does not seek her own, love thinketh no evil, for love rejoices not in inequities, but love rejoices in truth. Love hopeth all *things, endureth all things, beareth all things for love never failing, but where there is prophesies they shall fail, where there is tongues, they shall cease, where there is knowledge, it shall vanish away, and the last of those scriptures it says and now abideth hope, faith and love but the greatest of these three is love!'*

"I thank you very much, God bless you, and I love you!"

The memories of that day remain fresh with Lem. "Going back over all those years with the Lions and remembering the days when the crowd was cheering could only have been surpassed by those cheers after my acceptance speech at the Hall of Fame," he says.

"Today, when I go back to Canton, I'm asked to provide a few remarks about how blessed and how fortunate we are to be in this unique club. And most of the time, I'm asked to offer the prayer over lunch, I'm the invocator. So a lot of the things I would say to them, I would say openly to the Father. I tell new classes how blessed we are to have God-given talents and the ability to play our game. We are the greatest of the greatest. I am Ring Number 161 and I go back every year because it's a joy. I'm on a team consisting of all champions. The Lions never won the big one, but now I'm on a winning team for the rest of my life."

Going Home

"Home is where the heart is."

*H*OME MEANS DIFFERENT THINGS TO different people. Thomas Wolfe said, "You can never go home." Dorothy from the Wizard of Oz said, "There's no place like home."

Home for Lem has always meant the small, seaside town of Gulfport, Mississippi. That's where his story started, in the Barney home—a place where faith was preached, tolerance taught, and the dinner table was always set with portions of humility, hope, and faith, fresh off the menu.

At this humble castle, the only son of Lemuel and Berdell Barney was truly king—not of the Lions yet, but of the Barney home. "He's our only brother, and he was the king," says Lem's sister Varina. "We were raised in a Christian family and mother told us to always love one another because one day it's all you're going to have," Varina says. "And she was right. My parents' marriage was loving and we did a lot of family activities together. We played cards, went to the movies and Fats Domino concerts... But our favorite place—the place everyone would always want to visit—was our home cuz Mama was the best cook ever."

The smell of a mother's cooking—that might be the best definition of home. And in 1992, Lem's hometown of Gulfport was cooking up something special for their favorite son to honor his Hall of Fame induction. Everyone was there, and his mother and father were there in spirit.

Lem's only daughter, Latrece, remembers when her grandmother passed away. "I was 13 years old and extremely close to Grandmother when she passed," says Latrece. "It was extremely hard. She had spent all of her summers with us since the day we were born, and she was a huge part of our lives. Even though we were very young, we used to talk about how we feared my grandmother passing away. We thought that would be the first time we'd see our father break down and cry.

Latrece says that Lem was always the voice of reason and peace in the family and that he could always shine a light. "Because of his love for Grandmother," she says, "my brother and I always thought it would be so bad when she passed. The night it happened, our whole family broke down, but Dad kept his composure. I kept saying, 'Dad, I'm so sorry you lost your mom.' I was concerned he was trying to comfort us the best that he could, and we just kept thinking that he would break down any second.

"My father was a great singer. He was always perky and singing, even when he was taking me to the hairdresser before we went to Mississippi for the funeral. On this one particular day, we were driving and listening to music on the radio and for the first time in my life, I heard my father singing off key."

Latrece thought her father was crying through the song. But through the entire funeral service, he remained strong and she never saw him break down. "We figured that in private, he was mourning his loss in his own way. It was the same when his dad passed."

In 1992, when Lem was inducted into the Hall of Fame, Gulfport honored him with a celebration. "Different speakers were there to speak on his behalf," Latrece says. "I was going to surprise him by singing 'The Wind Beneath My Wings.'"

When Latrece took the stage, Lem was surprised. And as his daughter sang, she realized that she wouldn't be able to get through it without crying. "All of a sudden, my dad stood up took the microphone and held me as we both broke down and cried. That was the first and only time in my life that I had ever seen my father cry. I felt like his whole life just came full circle and he just let go. That's something I'll never forget as long as I live."

Everything truly had come full circle for Lem. He was the only one in his family to go to college, and Latrece says that he paved the way for all of them. "He took care of his family," she says. "He bought his mother a house and took care of them forever."

It's just another example of how Lem really is the wind beneath the wings of the Barney family.

Still Home After the Storm Katrina

*I*T DIDN'T LOOK LIKE HIS HOME. IT DIDN'T look like anybody's home anymore.

It didn't look like anything Lem Barney had ever seen in his life.

Hurricane Katrina had changed everything. It had done so in the most devastating way possible. With a brutal force of nature, Katrina had changed both the landscape and seascape drastically, perhaps forever, of a place that many still called home, but that few could now recognize.

Lem looked at the scene with disbelief. As a small boy, he had played on these beaches, fields, and streets. He played everywhere. Everywhere he played was his place. Now everywhere was out of place. He shook his head and hit his knees. Whenever words would leave him speechless, he would seek the Word. It was yet one more lesson that his mom taught him growing up—how to deal with the storms—the big storms that life brings.

"I remember riding the storms out as a boy with my mom and dad and my sisters," Lem says. "We didn't evacuate. We stayed and we prayed. That's what we always did."

Lem's parents had a routine where they would get their candles out, huddle around them, and pray through the storm. "We would stay together and pray together," he says.

With Katrina, Lem's sisters, who live in Gulfport, Mississippi, have had a change of heart about how to deal with storms.

"After Katrina, my sisters said that they have faith," Lem says. "But next time, they're moving to higher ground."

Over the years, the Barney family has been spared the wrath of many destructive storms. "They were very blessed this time," Lem says. "My sister's home was hardly damaged. Yet in so many areas I visited, the devastation was beyond description. It was like a war zone. So many places that I knew so well were unrecognizable."

As the storm approached his hometown, he lost contact with his family for five long days. To deal with the nervous days and the lack of communication with his family, Lem communicated with the Lord through prayer.

"The phones were down for days," he says. "There was no way to get through. I heard nothing from my sisters and my family. I did the only thing that I really can do—the only thing that any of us can do—I prayed for their safe passage through the storms."

Finally, one of Lem's nieces found a working cell phone and called to let him and Jacci know they were all safe. "Naturally, we were relieved," Lem says. "What a blessing."

Shortly thereafter, Lem visited the beleaguered Mississippi Gulf Coast area, as part of a contingent headed up by the Detroit Pistons, providing supplies, moral support, and, of course, prayers for a people and region in ruin.

"From what I saw when I visited the area, Katrina looked like a Category 6 or 7 when it hit land," Lem says. "I've seen what other hurricanes have done—including Camille. They were nothing like this. When you see what happened there, you just shake your head. It's so big. You see hundreds of homes completely destroyed, huge casinos moved, and people in so much pain."

To ease their pain, Lem offered a hand and his prayers.

"You see people and you just try to help," he says. "You see the pain in their eyes. They've all lost so much. The Lord has spared the people that have survived the storms. They have their lives. The areas will come back, and the people—while wounded—will come back, too. We don't know why some people survive and some people die, but the Lord knows. It's in his plan."

And Lem doesn't blame God for the destruction.

"A lot of people want to blame a lot of people. It's the blame game. Some people even want to blame God. But how can we know what's in his master plan?"

As far as the bureaucracy and the reaction of the governments at all levels, Lem looks at the big picture. "This was a huge storm," he says. "Some people didn't get out that should have gotten out. Relief should have come earlier. Mistakes were made at all levels. And some people in positions of power were not qualified. The President has vowed to rebuild the area, and I think he genuinely cares. He's saying the right things, and I think he'll walk the talk.

"Sadly, many people died in the storm. But gratefully, many more people were saved by heroic efforts of people who didn't care if someone was black or white, or rich or poor when they pulled them out of the water or rescued them from their rooftop."

Seeing the devastation of a place he still calls home saddens Lem. But it also strengthens his faith. And it takes him back to a time and place where his mother and father helped quarterback him through the many storms of life.

"When I was a little kid," he says, "we would stay and pray. We would say the Lord's Prayer and try to get through the storm. Sometimes the winds were so loud and so strong, they would howl."

As large projectiles hurtled toward the Barney house, Lem had an eerie feeling. "It was like being on a ride that you couldn't get off of—one you weren't sure would ever stop," he says. "The lights would be out. It was completely dark. The winds howled the rain would pour down on us."

But deep down, Lem knew he could count on the calming effect of the Lord.

"I can't say that I was really scared," he says. "Mom and Dad saw to it that we were staying and praying together. And that's how we got through it all."

Footsteps VI
The Gates of Heaven

The thin, old man made his way up the hill. He paused occasionally to look around. Looking only forward and never back, a soft smile graced his lips.

"Have I been here before?" he said quietly as the sun started to rise.

"My, it looks familiar. I could have sworn ... I mean it just feels like I've been here before. I just know it," he said softly under his breath to no one in particular. Because after all, there was no one else anywhere in sight on this deserted, yet friendly stretch of green grass that took the old man higher into the clouds.

Winded, but not tired from his journey, the old man suddenly became refreshed, almost reborn with a new sense of energy and wonder as he climbed farther up the hill. He had traveled for some time, yet now he showed no sign of fatigue. Invigorated and inspired by this leg of his journey, the old man focused on the road ahead. As he made his way down the road, he now moved at a brisker pace, better suited for a man of 20 than 80.

Higher and higher he climbed up the mountain. The bright morning sun was now shining directly in his eyes. Still, he did not blink. He merely took it in. He smiled, gave thanks, and said a little prayer on his way up the mountain road.

"The sun is good," he said. "All things are good under the sun. Thank you, Lord, for making this day and all the others in my life." The old man looked directly into the sun and smiled. It was a content, soft smile filled with wisdom, joy, and peace. He looked down at the ground and paused for a moment as a squirrel caught his eye. And then he looked up to the heavens. "And thank you, Lord, for filling so many of my days with an abundance of sunshine."

The old man continued to walk for hours, but he was not winded. He was not the least bit tired. In fact, he felt like he could go on forever. Just then a storm cloud settled in. The old man looked up at the clouds and smiled again. "It's a good thing I didn't wash my car," he thought to himself. Then he laughed at his little joke. In a matter of moments, he thought to himself, it would be coming down in buckets. Raining cats and dogs. Still, the thought did not dampen his mood or break his pace. He continued on.

And that's when it started. Slowly at first, but relentless all the same, snowflakes began their descent to the earth from above. At first, they came down in the form of small flakes. Then, they got bigger and bigger. Soon, they covered the once-green path that the old man was on. Soon the ground would be pure white.

The old man caught the snowflakes on his tongue as he danced in the fresh powder.

Smiling. Laughing. Carrying on like a child, the old man paused for a moment.

"This reminds me of that Thanksgiving Day game against the Vikings," he thought. "It snowed so hard, we couldn't see the ball. We couldn't keep our footing. We were slipping all over the place."

Again, a soft smile filled the old man's face.

"That's funny," he thought. "I don't feel cold at all."

Then he looked down at his feet. "That's funny," he thought. "I have great traction. I'm moving good, now. Best I've moved in years ...maybe ever."

As the snowflakes fell faster and harder, covering the old man's path, his pace quickened. Still, with the instincts of an old Lion, he followed the path onward and upward at a breakneck pace, pausing only to catch the occasional snowflake on his tongue. This pleased the old man greatly. He stopped by the side of the road and roared with laughter as he looked toward the heavens.

"I never knew this white stuff was so beautiful," he said aloud. "God, I love the snow."

Kneeling down in the snow, the old man broke into a conversation with his maker.

"Thank you, Lord, not only for the sunny days, but also the stormy ones. Thank you for all the days. Yes, indeed, seek and you shall find. You are right, my Lord. Thank you, Lord, for the snowstorms and the rain and for helping me weather everything."

The old man finished his prayer and started to get up. Then something stopped him. Something broke his concentration. He was frozen staring at the road ahead. The old man rose to his feet ever so slowly as he placed the black derby on his head. He retrieved his cane from a nearby snow pile. Then he threw it back in haste.

"I don't need this now," he thought to himself.

His focus remained on what was left of the road ahead. Suddenly, almost miraculously, the path had led him here. To some, it may have appeared a dead end. The old man knew it was not. He just looked ahead and stared. He was not afraid. He was not anxious. He was just here. Waiting. Staring. Hoping.

And praying. As he looked at the road that led to a large golden gate, adorned with flowers that he had never seen before, in colors that he had only dreamed. The old man opened his eyes wide and took the sight in. Magnificent hues of the rainbow filled his eyes and overwhelmed his heart. The old man fell to his knees and began to cry.

"Yes, my Lord, open your heart and eyes. Yes, my Lord, see things with the faith of a child ..." The old man got up with a newfound energy. Almost effortlessly, with his second wind, he took a step toward the gate. All the distance that he had traveled, in all the days of his life, had now come to this. The miles remaining on his journey had now been replaced with steps.

All that stood between the old man and the golden gate now was a short distance—one hundred yards.

The reflection of the flowers' brilliant colors mirrored a sunset as they almost blinded him. Calmly, the old man reached into his pocket and pulled out his sunglasses and affixed them to his head and his brilliantly animated face.

He started toward the gate.

Ten yards.

Then ten yards more.

Then another ten yards more and ten more yards.

"I'm almost there," he said. "Just fifty more yards."

The snow stopped falling as the old man continued on.

Just fifty more yards.

"I can do this with my eyes closed," he thought. "But I better keep them open."

The old man moved quickly now as his pace picked up.

Ten more yards—and another and another.

There were only twenty yards left.

The old man removed his glasses and threw his derby down in the snow.

"I'm going to sprint the final twenty," he said.

He paused and dropped to his knees. Gradually he got up and assumed a sprinter's stance. All the while, the old man remained focused on the gate that invited him forward. In position now, the old man with a lion's heart stared at the ground in deep concentration, awaiting only His direction from above on when to break for the gate.

In deep thought, the old man stared at the snow, which then began to melt. The old man could see beautiful, green grass again. He began to pray to himself and to the Lord.

"Lord, I'm ready," he said. "Lord, your humble servant is ready. I await your command."

The birds had stopped singing. The wind was still. And everything remained serene.

His was the only voice that he could hear now as he waited. Then the command came. The old man knew what to do.

And in an instant, he broke for the gate in a dead sprint. Again he heard His voice from above. It was loud and clear.

"You can do it. You can do anything. You can be anything. You are my son. You are supernatural."

The old man ran like never before toward the gate. Faster than he had ever run before, faster than a young lion, the old man flew toward the gate, his feet barely touching the ground.

"Just twenty more yards, Lord."

As he flew through the air, the old man counted off the last twenty yards of his journey.

Twenty, Nineteen, Eighteen, Seventeen, Sixteen, Fifteen, Fourteen, Thirteen, Twelve, Eleven, Ten, Nine, Eight, Seven, Six, Five, Four, Three, Two, One...

"I made it!" the old man cried as he crossed the flowery archway that preceded the golden gate. "I made it!"

The smell of fresh flowers overwhelmed his senses. The old man took it in. Inhaling all the glory and beauty of the blooms. A tear ran down his cheek. Slowly the gate began to open. The old man could hear only His voice.

"Lay not up for yourselves treasures upon earth, where moth and rust doth corrupt, and where thieves break through and steal. But lay up for yourselves treasures in heaven, where neither moth and rust doth corrupt and where thieves do not break through nor steal. For where your treasure is, there your heart will be also."

The gate opened a bit more as the old man approached.

The old man hung his head humbly toward the ground.

Tears of joy filled his eyes.

And again he listened as His voice called to him.

"Behold, I stand at the door and knock. If anyone hears My voice and opens the door, I will come unto him and dine with him and he with Me."

The golden gates opened up completely.

The old man lifted his head and headed toward the opening.

Slowly, reverently he passed through the gate.

Immediately, he fell to his knees and kissed the flower-filled ground and gave thanks.

"Thank you Lord, for everything great and small. And thank you for helping me through it all.

I am your faithful servant."

The old man wept with complete joy, contentment, and peace.

As he did, the gates behind him started to close.

And a young child turned back to look.

Through the gates, the boy gazed back at how far he had come on his life's journey. All of his footsteps were there, outlined in the sand, the grass, the mud, and the snow, except for the last twenty yards. Now he understood all there was to understand.

The boy smiled as he took a handful of rose, tulip, and gardenia petals and held them to his lips.

He roared with laughter, as only a child can. He lifted up the flowers with wonder, as only a child can. He sang at the top of his lungs, as only a child can. He bore a peaceful, innocent smile, as only a child can.

The old man was gone.

And in his place was a child.

He sat at his Father's table.

There he hungered for the Word.

The little boy was finally home.

"Well done, my good and faithful servant," said the Lord. "Well done."

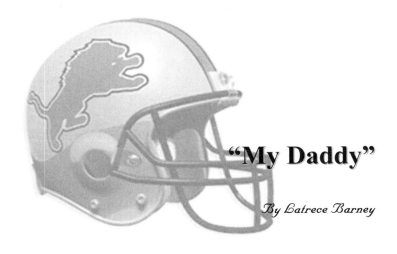

"My Daddy"

By Latrece Barney

You are sweeter than maple from a maple tree
Busier than a bumblebee
More original than the apple tree
That's what you are to me

Sunnier than the rising morning sun
Number one over all champions
Grandma could've named you "Fun"
Cuz that's what you are to me

You're better than the days when skies are blue
You're even more reliable than the truth
You are the definition of loyalty
You are to me

You're better than the best could ever be
To spell your name is simply L-O-V-E
You're deeper than the depths of every sea
You are to me

† Lem Barney †

More mystical than shooting stars will ever be
Better than presents under Christmas trees
Bigger then the entire galaxy
You are to me

More colorful than rainbows on a rainy day
Right directions after going the wrong way
Better than Shakespeare's finest play
That's what you are to me

Better than the days when skies are blue
Even more reliable than the truth
You're the definition of sincerity
Better than the best could ever be

Deeper than the depths of every sea
To spell your name is simply L-O-V-E
And that is my daddy!

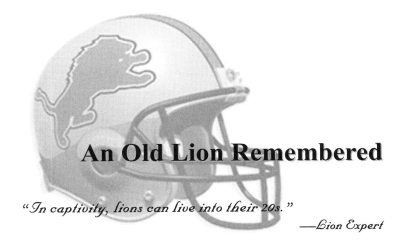

An Old Lion Remembered

"In captivity, lions can live into their 20s."

—*Lion Expert*

$\mathcal{A}$ VERY WISE SOUL WAS ONCE ASKED, "How do you want to be remembered?"

"I just want to be remembered," he answered.

Some of the dearest people to Lem Barney were asked that question about the man who, God willing, has many years left to play on this field.

Lem's two surviving sisters, Varina and Lemelda, say that he will be remembered as a great guy, a great father, a great brother and a great athlete. To know him, they say, is to love him—that is for sure.

Charlie Sanders will remember Lem's infectious, positive attitude. "He was never down, always outgoing, upbeat and positive, and full of energy" he says. "Lem probably had to deal with much more than most people understood, but he didn't show us that side of his life."

Former Secretary of Education Dr. Roderick Paige coached Lem in college, but believes Lem's legacy far exceeds his exploits on the gridiron. "His legacy will be one of a gifted human being who earned great respect from a wide range of sources—from opposing teams, adoring fans, and most of all, from his mother," Paige says. "She came to every game he played at Jackson State to provide encouragement and support. She even sent me a few thank you letters for coaching her son. Lem is somebody special and today's kids need to be made aware of his skills and character. I cannot tell you how proud I was watching him on television playing with the Lions and picking off Bart Starr's pass and taking it into the end zone. I still think of that moment today."

Monday Night Football legend and fellow Hall of Famer Frank Gifford thinks Lem is someone who touches the life of everyone he meets. "Lem will be remembered by everyone he ever met," Gifford says. "I first met Lem at the Hall of Fame ceremonies and have come to know and admire him more over the years. His spirituality and ministry is performed in a wonderful way. Lem is articulate, bright, and makes living fun."

It's his giving nature that makes Lem stand out in the mind of former NFL coach Don Shula. "I think he genuinely cares about people," Shula says. "That attribute is an integral part of his unique personality. He wants to know how you're doing and what's new in your life. That's a great quality to have."

Mel Renfro of the Dallas Cowboys says it's Lem's warm, welcoming ways that first come to mind, and his love of his fellow man. "Every time I see him, he greets me with a hug and nobody else in my life does that," Renfro says. "I appreciate him so much because he lifts me up."

Former Baltimore Colts star Lenny Moore thinks Lem gave the planet as much as he gave the game of football. "I will always remember him as a great ballplayer and a greater human being," Moore says. "The world needs what he has to offer. What he brings to the table for us to feast on is far beyond what we came to the table initially for. That's what we get from Lem every time we're around him. He has a great ministry. That is his calling."

Lem will be remembered for many things, some of which he will hopefully still accomplish in the coming years. One thing remains clear; when they sum up the life of one Lemuel Barney, he will be remembered for:

How he walked and talked.

How he ran up and down the field.

How he dreamed and how accomplished his dreams.
How he won and how he lost.
How he got up after he fell.
How he was a brother to all.
How he loved.

"I want to be remembered as a servant to others," Lem says. "I came to serve—that's my greatest joy. For my epitaph, I would like the lines from that copper Rotary Club coin: *Service above self.*"

> *"Lives of great men all remind us*
> *We can make our lives sublime*
> *And, departing, leave behind us*
> *Footprints on the sand of time."*
>
> —*Henry Wadsworth Longfellow*

... STATISTICS ...

PLAYING STATISTICS

SEASON	TEAM(S)	GAMES	DEFENSE				FUMBLES	TOTAL
			INT	YDS	AVG	TD		POINTS
1967		14	10	232	23.2	3	2	18
1968	DET	14	7	82	11.7	0	5	6
1969	DET	13	8	126	15.8	0	3	6
1970	DET	13	7	168	24	2	2	18
1971	DET	9	3	78	26	1	5	6
1972	DET	14	3	88	29.3	0	1	0
1973	DET	14	4	130	32.5	0	3	0
1974	DET	13	4	61	15.3	0	0	0
1975	DET	10	5	23	4.6	0	0	0
1976	DET	14	2	62	31	1	4	6
1977	DET	12	3	27	9	0	0	0
CAREER		140	56	1,077	19.2	7	25	60

SEASON	TEAM(S)	PUNT RET.				KICK RET.			
		PR	YDS	AVG	TD	KR	YDS	AVG	TD
1967	DET	4	14	3.5	0	5	87	17.4	0
1968	DET	13	79	6.1	0	25	670	26.8	1
1969	DET	9	191	21.2	1	7	154	22	0
1970	DET	25	259	10.4	1	2	96	48	0
1971	DET	14	122	8.7	0	9	222	24.7	0
1972	DET	15	108	7.2	0	1	17	17	0
1973	DET	27	231	8.6	0	1	28	28	0
1974	DET	5	37	7.4	0				
1975	DET	8	80	10	0				
1976	DET	23	191	8.3	0				
Career		143	1,312	9.2	2	50	1,274	25.5	1

HONORS, AWARDS
...AND AFFILIATIONS...

➤ **Named Defensive Rookie Of The Year- 1967**
- ▷ League High Of 10 Interceptions
- ▷ Returned 3 Interceptions For Touchdowns
- ▷ Intercepted First Pass Thrown In His Direction As NFL Player
- ▷ Earned A Berth On The All-Pro Team & A Trip To The Pro Bowl
- ▷ Intercepted 56 Passes (2nd In Lions History)
- ▷ Returned 7 Interceptions For Touchdowns
- ▷ Played In The Pro Bowl 7 Of 11 Seasons
- ▷ Named All-Pro 7 Years
- ▷ Gained 1,079 Yards On Interception Returns
- ▷ All-Time Leader In Yards Returned On Interceptions
- ▷ Named Most Valuable Player In 1967 & 1968
- ▷ All Time Leader In Punt Returns With 143 For 1,312 Yards
- ▷ Total Yards Gained Defensively B 4,000
- ▷ Voted Team Captain 7 Years

➤ **Lem's Outstanding Career Has Earned Him A Spot In Several Halls Of Fame:**
- ▷ Detroit Lions Hall Of Fame
- ▷ Jackson State University Hall Of Fame
- ▷ Michigan Hall Of Fame
- ▷ Mississippi Sports Hall Of Fame
- ▷ Blue Grey Hall Of Fame
- ▷ International Afro-American Hall Of Fame
- ▷ NFL Hall Of Fame - Class Of 1992

HONORS
- ▷ Selected as one of the Outstanding Young Men of America,
- ▷ 1969, 1973 and 1987.
- ▷ Selected in The Sporting News as one of the All Time Greatest Players 1999
- ▷ Selected one of the top 20, Detroit 300 Sports Players - #13-2001
- ▷ Selected as one of NFL's All-Time Greatest Players - 2000

247

Vocal Albums:

- ▷ "What's Going On" • Marvin Gaye • Motown Records • Received Gold Record

Clubs. Foundations. Charities.

- ▷ Boy Scouts of America
- ▷ Dough Hoffman, Ltd. Diabetes Association
- ▷ Floyd Rice Ford Michigan Career Foundation
- ▷ March of Dimes Fire Prevention
- ▷ NAACP Voting Rights
- ▷ Black United Fund United Negro College Fund
- ▷ Chamber of Commerce City of Detroit
- ▷ Associate Minister with Springhill Missionary Baptist Church
- ▷ Board of Directors: Better Education Through Simplified Spelling
- ▷ Detroit Institute for Children
- ▷ Goodwill Industries
- ▷ Neighborhood Renaissance
- ▷ Old Newsboys/Goodfellows
- ▷ Omni Arts in Education
- ▷ Prison Fellowship B National Rehabilitation Consultant
- ▷ National Football Hall of Fame Alumni
- ▷ Board of Trustees: Boy Scouts of America
- ▷ Franklin Wright Settlements
- ▷ Metro Detroit Youth Foundation
- ▷ United Way
- ▷ Advisory Board: Joy of Jesus, Inc.
- ▷ Youth Day/ City of Detroit
- ▷ Board Member: Goodwill Industries of Greater Detroit
- ▷ National Football League Alumni Association
- ▷ New Detroit Racial & Economic Justice Committee
- ▷ 1987 Adopt-a-Child
- ▷ Detroit Osteopathic Hospital
- ▷ Chamber of Commerce—Highland Park
- ▷ Chamber of Commerce—Hamtramck
- ▷ For Our Children
- ▷ Jackson State Alumni—Detroit Chapter
- ▷ State of Michigan Sports Hall of Fame

- ▷ Eastwood Clinics Substance Abuse
- ▷ Horizon Health Systems—Foundation
- ▷ Volunteers In Prevention, Probation & Prisons
- ▷ Chairman: Detroit Metro Prison Fellowship Care Committee
- ▷ Chairman Emeritus: Partners Program
- ▷ Lifetime Member: National Association for the Advancement of Colored People
- ▷ Kappa Alpha Phi Fraternity
- ▷ Volunteer Work: Active volunteer for community-based programs
- ▷ March of Dimes
- ▷ Special Olympics
- ▷ Michigan Blind Foundation
- ▷ Cystic Fibrosis Foundation
- ▷ Todd-Phillips Home
- ▷ Detroit Lions Alumni
- ▷ Easter Seal Telethon
- ▷ United Negro College Fund Telethon

MILITARY
- ▷ United States Naval Reserves B 1967 B 1969 (Seaman)

HOBBIES:
- ▷ Golf
- ▷ Tennis
- ▷ Racquetball
- ▷ Swimming
- ▷ Jogging
- ▷ Dancing
- ▷ Acting
- ▷ Model
- ▷ Carpentry
- ▷ Billiards
- ▷ Singing

$\mathcal{I}$MMORTAL INVESTMENTS PUBLISHING would like to thank the following individuals and organizations for their participation in this publication. Without you, the Lem Barney story would have been incomplete.

The King James Bible
The Detroit Lions
The Pro Football Hall of Fame
The Detroit News
The Detroit Free Press
Lem Barney
Jacci Barney
Lemuel Barney III
Latrece Barney
Varina Barney
Lemelda Barney
Martha Barney
Dave Bing
Mel Farr
Dr. Roderick Paige
Billy Sims
Tim Pendell
Dave Mesrey
Charlie Sanders
Dick Jauron
Mike Weger
Jim Acho
Joe Hoskins
Benny White
Jerry Berry
Jim Thrower
Will Robinson
The late, great Joe Falls
Jerry Green
Mike O'Hara
Dr. Willie Farmer
Pastor. Ronald G. Arthur
Joe Schmidt
Barry Sanders
Gale Sayers
Bob Griese

Lynn Swann
Don Maynard
Lance Alworth
Deacon Jones
Mel Blount
Jack Ham
Ted Hendricks
Willie Lanier
Lou Creekmur
William Dudley
Willie Davis
Stan Jones
Willie Wood
Ronnie Lott
Jim Taylor
Ozzie Newsome
Lenny Moore
Mel Renfro
Paul Krause
Ken Houston
Leroy Kelly
Y.A. Tittle
Frank Gifford
Bobby Mitchell
Don Shula
Marcus Allen
Roger Staubach
Bart Starr
Dr. Bill Cosby
Del Reddy
Dennis Fassett
Jill B. Thomas

A MESSAGE FROM THE PUBLISHER

We are very proud to present the extraordinary story of the legendary Lem Barney in *The Supernatural*. Gus Mollasis has artfully crafted the remarkable life of one of Detroit's all time favorite sport's heroes. We are supremely grateful to Lem and his lovely wife, Jacci. Also, we appreciate the Detroit Lions and other special friends for their unique input and participation. Immortal Investments is honored to present *The Supernatural*. It will inspire readers now and in future generations. God Bless!

Michael J. Reddy
Publisher

Immortal Investments Publishing produces timeless books that move, inspire, and spotlight the best of the human spirit manifested by extraordinary human achievement.

Please review and order our other outstanding titles by visiting www.immortalinvestments.com or by calling **1-800-475-2066.**

Please let us know if you have suggestions for other exceptional books or have comments about *The Supernatural.*

***This publishing venture is revolutionary in that the book like all other Immortal Investment titles is not distributed to bookstores. It is available exclusively through Immortal Investments Publishing.

To bring Lem Barney to your event for a personal book signing please contact www.immortalinvestments.com.

Order your signed copy by
Lem Barney today!
1-800-475-2066.
NOT SOLD IN BOOKSTORES

Immortal Investmants Publishing
35122 W. Michigan Ave. Wayne, MI 48184

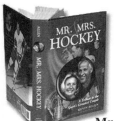
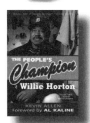

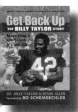

boji books PRESENTS...

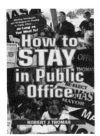